PRAISE FOR DAVID J. WALLACE AND

"Once you pick up *The Journey of Our Souls*, you will not be able to put it down. Kahu Dave's experiences have helped to mold him into the person he has become today. You will be absorbed by his accounts and want to know where it all leads. Enjoy the journey!"

— Stephania Gibb, Author of *Don't Throw Your Firstborn (or Yourself) Off the Balcony*

"*The Journey of Our Souls* is profound, powerful, beautifully written, enlightening, engaging, and so much more. It is an important source that will aid so many people. David's sharing of his experiences helped me tremendously. This book will allow many of my young students who have spiritual gifts to embrace, develop, and use them."

— Karen Loebl Kaulana, Host of the Radio Show *Healing Hawaii with Karen Kaulana*

"It was an honor and a privilege to receive the Ha Ki'i Reset from David! It was so wonderful, so magical, so awesome! I felt my ancestors, my kupuna, my 'aumakua, past, present, and future, as well as David's were all there to participate, protect, and guide us through the process! It was truly intense! Very emotional! Such a feeling of release!"

— Keala Tolbert, LMT

"Kahu Dave is an excellent Kumu (teacher), and his methods are truly clear and easy to learn. I also enjoyed being outdoors when attending his class because being in a natural environment opens my ability to take in something new so much more."

— Jeffery Bow, Author of *Stop Thinking, Start Believing*

"Recently, Dave did a reading for me and was accurate with things from my past. For obvious reasons then, I am so looking forward to his near future predictions for me—job, money."

— Phyllis Wong, Counselor

"David is a down-to-earth soul who has a most loving and caring heart! He gave me both sides of the coin so I could adjust my life to what is needed for my spiritual growth. He is a humble person who uses his own life lessons and experiences to better explain a few things. Thank you, Kahu Dave, for your guidance!"

— Karen Cadabona, LMT

"Very touched, inspired, and soul-filled awe…your near-death experiences and everything associated with them grabbed my heart. What you have experienced, endured, gathered strength in, embraced, and mastered. I am in awe and filled with a deeper sense of your gifts, our ancestors, your spiritual bonds/guidance, and Heavenly Father's true love for you. It was such a wonderful honor to read your writings."

— Rayma Laufou, Staffing Consultant, Employment Options

"This was a very compelling read. Strange the things we must go through to get to the light. I like how your kupuna (ancestors) had to help you twice with demonic influences. It is kind of like the bitter medicine we hate to take because it tastes awful, but it is what we need to heal us. Much respect and admiration, Kahu. This book reads like a bestseller!"

— Robert Lopaka Kapanui, Owner, Mysteries of Honolulu

"Kahu David Wallace's Ha Ki'i class is excellent for those interested in learning how to use their intuition and identify areas in the body that may require attention. This class is taught in an easy-to-understand way whether you are a beginner or have had experience in energetic work."

— Robbi Aranita, Energy Healer

"David is a teacher who connects from the heart with each student. He has the natural ability to bring out each student's gifts. I had so much fun learning, connecting, and growing. I cannot wait for the next class!"

— Kathy Caranza, Psychic Reader

"I appreciate David's strong connection to the island and his active communication with his ancestors. His diverse spiritual background, natural gifts, and training helped me get through some difficult times."

— Brandy Davis, Educator

"I am beyond grateful for all the guidance, support, love, and respect I have received from Kahu Dave! He has shown me a new perspective."

— Suzy Marshall, Flight Attendant

"David has helped me identify what I am feeling and sensing. Because of that, I am more confident in identifying the feelings, dreams, and visions I get. He gave my daughter and me a precious gift...he opened our hands to feeling energy."

— Josie Rodrigues, Medium

"I had a reading with Dave Wallace today. He was really on point with everything he said. He knew things only I would know. He listened, had patience, and did not rush through the conversation. He made sure I understood his answers and that he also understood me."

— Lahela Keliikuli, Tax Preparer

"Dave's gifts, intuition, and guidance have been such an amazing experience for my husband and me. He has always been spot-on and helped us grow with his insights in so many areas. We feel so blessed and thankful."

— Maile Kawakami, Realtor

"In *The Journey of Our Souls,* David Wallace reveals that we can create our own destinies in surprising ways, especially when our ancestors step in to help us. His mind-blowing story of coming back from the dead and his advice for healing your life physically and spiritually will make you a believer in the power of the Universe and its many mysteries."

— Patrick Snow, Publishing Coach and Best-Selling Author of *Creating Your Own Destiny* and *Boy Entrepreneur*

"I thank the planets for aligning to bring David and his family into my life every day. His insight and ties to his ancestral lineage are profound. His readings are incredibly accurate, and his heart and care for the world is in a class of its own."

— Maria Torres, Energy Healer

"In *The Journey of Our Souls*, David Wallace recounts his four amazing near-death experiences, as well as his vast knowledge about Hawaiian culture and spiritual traditions. This is a man deeply in touch with his ancestors as well as the spiritual realm. This book will leave people seeing life and its purpose in a new light."

— Tyler R. Tichelaar, PhD and Award-Winning Author of *The Gothic Wanderer* and *The Best Place*

"David Wallace is deeply in touch with the truths often hidden from the rest of us. In *The Journey of Our Souls*, his series of near-death experiences and his connection to his Hawaiian spiritual heritage not only make for a gripping read, but they reveal messages we all need to hear and instill in ourselves to make healthy, lasting changes."

— Nicole Gabriel, Author of *Finding Your Inner Truth* and *Stepping Into Your Becoming*

FREE GUIDES TO HEALING AND PREDICTING YOUR FUTURE INCLUDED

THE JOURNEY OF OUR Souls

WHAT YOU CAN LEARN FROM ONE MAN'S MULTIPLE NEAR-DEATH EXPERIENCES

DAVID J. WALLACE

AVIVA PUBLISHING
New York

The Journey of Our Souls: What You Can Learn from One Man's Multiple Near-Death Experiences

Copyright © 2020 by David J. Wallace. All rights reserved.

Published by:
Aviva Publishing
Lake Placid, NY
(518) 523-1320
www.AvivaPublishing

All Rights Reserved. No part of this book may be used or reproduced in any manner whatsoever without the expressed written permission of the author. Address all inquiries to:

David J. Wallace
1796 Eames Street
Wahiawa, HI 96786
(808) 349-4788
DavidJWallace04@gmail.com
TheJourneyofOurSouls.com

ISBN: 1-978-1-890427-42-9 (hard cover)
        978-0-578-74053-9 (eBook)
Library of Congress Control Number: 2020908159

Editor: Tyler Tichelaar, Superior Book Productions
Cover Design and Interior Layout: Nicole Gabriel, Angel Dog Productions
Author Photo Credit: Ellen Wallace

Every attempt has been made to properly source all quotes.

Printed in the United States of America

I dedicate this book to my ancestors and spirit guides who have blessed me with their patience and love while protecting my life so that I could become the person I am today. Some of these ancestors choose to remain nameless, but the key individuals who contributed to my development are my grandmother Ellen Wallace, ʻAumakua Pukonanui, and my primary teacher and adviser Hewahewa. While other family members have come to my aid when I needed their specific talents, these three individuals are always with me, protecting my back. Without their guidance, my life would be quite different.

Mahalo nui loa. Thank you very much for your help.

ACKNOWLEDGMENTS

I owe a debt of gratitude to the following people who helped me along my soul's journey and contributed to my development along the way. *Mahalo nui loa.* Thank you very much!

Kamanaʻopono Aweau Agres

Douglas Kaiwi Ah Hee

Dick Allgire

Reni ʻAi ʻAi Bello

Dr. Courtney Brown

Judith Conroy

James Ferla

Uncle Roy Goya

Robert Lopaka Kapanui

Rayma Laufou

Peter Lonoaea

Steve Nelli

Rodger Orlich

"Cowboy" Otsuka

Maureen O'Shaughnessy

Susan Stanton

Debra Duggan Takagi

Ellen Wallace

Glenn Wheaton

CONTENTS

A Note to the Reader		15
Introduction	Seeking Balance, Finding Peace	17
Chapter 1	Surviving My First NDE	21
Chapter 2	Seeing Spirits and Hidden Objects	33
Chapter 3	Clashing of Cultures	47
Chapter 4	Dreaming and Prophecy	61
Chapter 5	NDE 2: Finding Heaven	75
Chapter 6	Talking with Your Ancestors	87
Chapter 7	NDE 3: Meeting Death	101
Chapter 8	Becoming a Healer	111
Chapter 9	Becoming a Remote Viewer	125
Chapter 10	NDE 4: Finding Your Purpose in Life	139
Chapter 11	Becoming a Kahu	151
Chapter 12	Ha Ki'i Healing	163
Chapter 13	Ha Ki'i Medical Intuition	183
Chapter 14	Predicting Your Future	195
Chapter 15	Living as a Kahu and Psychic	211
Chapter 16	Being the Reluctant Leader	227
A Final Note		243
About the Author		247
About David J. Wallace's Coaching Program		249
Seminars, Workshops, and Training		251
Book Kahu David J. Wallace to Speak at Your Next Event		255

A NOTE TO THE READER

Portions of this book serve as a supplement to my workshops and seminars. These workshops and seminars focus on Ha Ki'i Healing, Ha Ki'i Medical Intuition, and Predicting Sporting Events. I have also changed the names of certain individuals to protect their identity and privacy.

Chapter 12 contains a copy of my manual for my Ha Ki'i Healing workshop. During this workshop, you will learn to use a pure form of healing energy to heal yourself and others. You will also learn to create and use a Healing Circle that is comprised of specific healing partners. The techniques you learn in this chapter will help you expand your own healing practices.

Chapter 13 reviews some of the important protocols we use in Ha Ki'i Medical Intuition. During this two-day workshop, you will learn to read the flow of energy to locate and detect injury or illness in a human. You will learn techniques that are part of the reiki and remote viewing disciplines that will enhance your development as a medical intuitive. This chapter is intended for people who want to develop their natural abilities to perform medical intuitive readings. The material in this chapter will help you develop a systematic approach to your medical intuitive practice.

Chapter 14 contains a copy of my Picking Winner$ workshop that focuses on predicting sporting events. During this workshop, you will learn to use an associative remote viewing method I use to accurately predict the outcome of any sporting event. This technique can be used to pick stocks, commodities, and investments. This chapter is intended for those who want to make accurate sports picks to improve their winnings.

INTRODUCTION

SEEKING BALANCE, FINDING PEACE

Have you ever considered how frustrating it is to be an immortal soul trapped inside your human body? Here you are, an enlightened being who will never taste death, partnered with a temporary home that was designed to eventually weaken, collapse, and die. It is like giving a world champion race car driver a secondhand beater with bald tires to compete in the Indianapolis 500. It is a disaster waiting to happen. This gap between spiritual potential and physical reality can create a lifetime of challenges as the soul, mind, and body attempt to coexist peacefully. This is not a simple task.

In many cultures, the soul is considered your moral compass that knows the difference between right or wrong. It is the beacon that guides you through the many journeys you experience in your lifetime. These journeys of your soul equip you with the tools and experiences you need to achieve balance and fulfillment. When you are out of balance and not living to your higher soul purpose, you begin to experience pain and discomfort.

Are you happy and content with the life you are leading right now? Are your soul, mind, and body working together in harmony, or are they in conflict with each other? Do you sense that something is missing from your life? Do you feel an urgency to make some changes, but you do not know where to start?

I understand your frustration. My struggles to find that perfect balance between my inflated ego and soul purpose have caused me much pain and suffering for most of my life. Years of development, coaxing, and four near-death experiences (NDEs) were required for me to reach a balance I am happy with.

In this book, you will learn about the different types of journeys your soul can attract to your life to create the person you were meant to be. You will learn that near-death experiences are gateways to developing new spiritual abilities and insights. You will understand how my first NDE triggered my ability to communicate with spirits and see objects hidden from view. You will discover how you can develop your natural talents and abilities and expand them to other areas. You will then learn, through the story of my second NDE, that a place called heaven exists where you can be reunited with your family and pets. After establishing contact with your ancestors and knowing who they are, you will learn ways you can talk with them if you so desire. Through my third NDE, you will learn that death is not as final as you may think. Many times, you need to face death to appreciate the life you have. You will then be introduced to concepts of energy healing and remote viewing. Through my fourth and final NDE, you will learn the important role of your spirit guides in protecting you when you are spiritually and physically threatened. In this book's closing sections, I will include some instructional materials for Ha Ki'i Healing and Medical Intuition, as well as a method I use to make predictions on sporting events. I will then end by sharing my work as a kahu (steward/caretaker) and psychic as well as my personal approach to leadership.

Our soul journeys are individual experiences, but if you take the lessons I learned through my own journey and apply some of them to your life, you could learn to achieve balance and fulfillment. The soul journey is a process, not a destination, that continues to shape and form our lives.

I do not profess to know all the answers to resolve all the personal issues you face. What I do have is a lifetime of experiences, insights, and skills that could help you navigate your soul journey. I am a natural clairvoyant whose skills have been enhanced by my training as a remote viewer. When you pair this ability with my prophetic dreams and visions, there are not many things that occur without me knowing beforehand. This knowledge helps me when I am assessing my clients' needs. I am also a retired teacher of twenty-six years; most of my years were spent working with special needs students. Developing hidden skills and talents in people is one of my strengths as a teacher and coach. Finally, my connection with my ancestors, spirit guides, and the natural energies around me allows me to share the same connectivity with my students. I am a reiki master, remote viewer, medical intuitive, healer, seer, professional psychic, ordained minister, and Native Hawaiian cultural practitioner. I will use all my skills and abilities to serve you.

I understand why you have hesitated to develop your own skills up to this point. Often, life interferes with our soul purpose and we lose focus. I have experienced many moments when I lost focus. Delaying your happiness and fulfillment just prolongs the stagnation you are currently experiencing. It is time to step outside of your shell and make the breakthroughs you desperately need.

Making changes can be very scary and challenging if you try to do this alone. Let me be your accountability partner and help coach you to achieve your goals. I want to be your mentor, guide, and friend. I want to celebrate your successes and calm your fears when times get tough. Let us work together to overcome your challenges.

Are you ready to expand your comfort zone and step into the new person you always dreamed about being? Are you ready to achieve your most precious goals, which have been eluding you all these years? If so, let us get started on your soul journey together and begin your transformation now.

CHAPTER 1
SURVIVING MY FIRST NDE

> "To fear death is nothing other than to think oneself wise when one is not. For it is to think one knows what one does not know. No one knows whether death may not even turn out to be one of the greatest blessings of human beings. And yet people fear it as if they knew for certain it is the greatest evil."
>
> — Socrates

The near-death experience (NDE) is a strange human experience that reaches far into our ancient beginnings. While thousands of people have experienced at least one NDE, very few have endured and survived multiple NDEs. I have survived four of them. In this chapter, we will examine the nature of an NDE—what it is, and what normally occurs during one. If you have experienced your own NDE, this chapter will help you compare your experience with others' experiences. We will then examine my first NDE, which occurred when I was five. Next, we will look at the NDEs of two celebrities. We will conclude this chapter by comparing my own NDE with the NDE characteristics reported by the International Association for Near Death Studies.

What is a near-death experience?

The International Association for Near Death Studies (IANDS) suggests that:

[a] near-death experience, or NDE, is a profound psychological event that may occur to a person close to death or who is not near death but in a situation of physical or emotional crisis. Being in a life-threatening situation does not, by itself, constitute a near-death experience. It is the pattern of perceptions, creating a recognizable overall event, that has been called "near-death experience."[1]

To qualify an event as a near-death experience does not require a person to die. According to IANDS, an NDE can occur when a person is on the brink of death or experiencing a physical or emotional crisis. Under those guidelines, all four events I experienced qualify as NDEs.

What are some common traits of an NDE?

IANDS identifies several common traits shared by people experiencing an NDE. Here are a few of them.

- A perception of seeing one's body from above (called an out-of-body experience, or OBE), sometimes watching medical resuscitation efforts or moving instantaneously to other places.
- A sense of being "somewhere else," in a landscape that may seem like a spiritual realm or world.
- Encountering deceased loved ones or possibly sacred figures (the Judges, Jesus, a saint) or unrecognized beings with whom communication is mind-to-mind; these figures may seem consoling, loving, or terrifying.
- A sensation of floating out of one's body. Often followed by an out-of-body experience where all that goes on around the "vacated" body is both seen and heard accurately.
- Passing through a dark tunnel or black hole or encountering darkness. This is often accompanied by a feeling or sensation of

1 https://www.iands.org/ndes/about-ndes/characteristics.html

movement or acceleration. Wind may be heard or felt.
- Ascending toward a light at the end of the darkness. A light of incredible brilliance, with the possibility of seeing people, animals, plants, lush outdoors, and even cities within the light.
- Being greeted by friendly voices, people, or beings who may be strangers, loved ones, or religious figures. Conversation can ensue; information or a message may be given.[2]

Each of the four NDEs I experienced involved one or more of the above elements.

My first NDE

I was a normal five-year-old child living a normal life on the island of Molokai, Hawaii. I was not aware that I had any special gifts or abilities. Then my whole life changed one day when Aunty Bertha took my brother Bill and me for a ride in our family car. Those were the early days before seatbelts were invented, so we were not strapped safely onto the seats. Bill and I started to roughhouse with each other in the backseat, wrestling and shoving each other around as brothers sometimes do. When I jumped on Bill, he kicked me so hard I flew backwards and hit the car door on the vehicle's opposite side. Slamming into the door, I grabbed its handle and pushed down to brace myself. Car doors opened by pushing down on the handle back then, so I flew out of the car just as my aunt made a turn. I landed headfirst onto the asphalt road.

NDE begins

I do not remember feeling any pain, but I immediately noticed something strange was happening. I found myself floating in the air, hovering over my body, and looking down at myself as if I were staring

---
[2] https://www.iands.org/ndes/about-ndes/characteristics.html

into a strange mirror. I could see some blood running from my nose with more blood collecting around the back of my head. I was terrified and tried to wake myself up, but I found I could not. As my fear turned to panic, I began to see shadows and lights swirling around me, as if I were caught in a whirlwind.

Suddenly, a large muscular arm wrapped around my waist, lifting me up and away from my body. I looked over my shoulder to see who had grabbed me and saw a huge Hawaiian man with a kind face. He looked at me, nodded, and smiled. I nodded and smiled back. Looking into his eyes gave me a warm, safe feeling. He was someone I felt I could trust.

We floated above the accident scene for a few seconds, but in an instant, we shot upward at a high rate of speed. We then entered a long dark tunnel where light and darkness zipped by us like passing cars in the night.

We finally arrived within a small room shaped like an octagon about twelve feet from wall to wall. Each side of the room had a door with a small glass window. The floor appeared to be made of cement. Above us was a bright shining light that filled the room with a soothing warmth. The light had a calming effect on me. I felt safe. Beyond the room was darkness, with only small portions of the exterior illuminated by the light emanating from the room.

Suddenly, I noticed movement outside. Curious, I walked toward one of the windows until my Hawaiian guardian grabbed my hand and said:

"No. Stay here."

I quickly sat down, not wanting to upset him.

Voices from beyond the room then began to call out to me:

"David John, come here; we miss you!"

Glancing at the windows, I saw familiar faces pressed against the glass. I stood up and dashed toward the door, but I was tackled from behind by my guardian. He then sat on my back and pressed me to the floor.

"I said, 'No!'" he repeated. "Stay here and do not open any of the doors!"

I struggled to push him off me, but I felt as though a baby elephant had decided to take a nap on me.

"Get off of me!" I yelled.

"Not until you promise not to open any of these doors."

Why was this man so insistent about my not opening the doors? Where was I? As I sorted through my thoughts about my situation, my guardian began to laugh as if he could read my mind.

"Don't worry, Imaikalani. You are in a safe place. I will make sure no one harms you while you are here."

"Am I in heaven?"

"No, this is not heaven. This is more of a waiting room."

"What are we waiting for?"

"We are waiting for your body to accept you back."

"Am I dead?"

"Not, really. Kind of in between."

The voices from beyond the room grew louder and more demanding. Soon they began to drown out our conversation.

"Who are all those people?" I asked my guardian.

"Good question. They are not who you think they are. They are tricksters who want to take you away and leave you wandering in the dark like them."

"But they look like some of my family members. They even know my name, so they must know me," I argued.

"Sure, they know you. But if you look at them with your spiritual eyes instead of your physical eyes, you will see clearly what they really are."

"How do I see with my spiritual eyes?" I asked.

"Just close your eyes and see with your mind's eye. Try it now."

I gazed at the many faces in the window and selected one individual who looked remarkably familiar. As I closed my eyes, the friendly face suddenly morphed into a demon! Startled, I popped open my eyes and realized I could now see the true nature of all the beings crowding the windows. They were all demons, hideous and frightening. As fear began to grip me, the light above the room glowed stronger and brighter. The brilliance of the light forced the demons away from the windows. I turned to my guardian with newfound respect.

"Thank you for helping me and keeping me safe. Who are you, anyway?"

The man chuckled.

"I am Kupuna,[3] an ancestor of yours."

Kupuna and I engaged in a variety of small talk as we waited in the room. He grew serious when he began to explain the various meanings behind my Hawaiian name Imaikalani. I realized I needed to pay close attention because he was sharing something particularly important with me.

I had always thought my name meant "I come from heaven," but Kupuna reminded me that Hawaiian names have many hidden mean-

---

3 Kupuna means "ancestor" in Hawaiian. In this case, Kupuna presented himself as an ancestor of mine. Throughout the rest of the book, I will refer to my kupuna (ancestors) collectively.

ings, almost like the layers of an onion. He told me that as I grew older, the hidden meanings behind my name would be revealed. Sacred names like mine evolved over time. As a child, Imaikalani describes a person who can communicate with heavenly beings, such as God, angels, ancestors, and spirits. In this phase of my life, I needed to learn how to see, talk, and listen to heavenly messengers. I would learn things faster if I listened to them.

Suddenly, I felt very tired. I snuggled up to Kupuna, who cradled me in his arms, and I fell into a deep, dreamless sleep.

As I slept, a strange sensation came over me. Suddenly, I was moving again, then falling from the sky. Startled, I suddenly woke up on a gurney and discovered I was being wheeled into an examination room. *Where am I? Am I in a hospital?* Pain slammed into me with an anguishing kick to the head. My skull ached and throbbed wretchedly, making me feel weak and dizzy. I slowly opened my eyes, making eye contact with the people trying to help me. The doctor and nurses were overly excited that I had regained consciousness.

Famous people who experienced NDEs

Historians have recorded stories of NDEs involving people from their time periods. The most famous of these ancient stories, "The Myth of Er," is in Plato's *Republic*. Er was a Greek soldier who was mortally wounded during battle. When his body was recovered, after several days on the field, it was noted his body had not decomposed like those of the rest of his slain companions. Ten days after being killed in battle, this soldier woke on his funeral pyre. Er went on to describe his journey through the afterlife.

In modern times, several celebrities have reported their own near-death experiences. Here are two examples:

Jane Seymour

When Jane Seymour was thirty-six, she had a severe case of the flu and was given an injection of penicillin. She suffered an allergic reaction to the penicillin, which led to a near-death experience. She reported that she literally left her body and could see herself on the bed, with people grouped around her. People were trying to resuscitate her. Seymour found herself hovering above them in the corner of the room, looking down. She saw people putting needles in her, trying to hold her down. She remembers her whole life flashing before her eyes. The only thing Seymour cared about was that she wanted to live because she did not want anyone else looking after her children. She was floating up there, thinking, "No, I don't want to die. I'm not ready to leave my kids." And that was when she said to God, "If you're there, God, if you really exist and I survive, I will never take your name in vain again." Seymour can remember pleading with the doctor to bring her back. She was determined not to die.

Peter Sellers

In 1964, Peter Sellers experienced the first of eight heart attacks. When his heart stopped, he was clinically dead. He had an out-of-body experience and saw the bright, loving light. Sellers felt himself leave his body, floating out of his physical form. He saw them cart his body away to the hospital. He followed his body into the hospital. Sellers was not frightened or anything like that because he felt fine; it was his body that was in trouble. He looked around and saw an incredibly beautiful, bright, loving white light above him. He wanted to go to that white light more than anything. Sellers knew there was love, real love, on the other side of the light, which was attracting him so much. It was kind and loving and he remembers thinking "That's God."[4]

---

4 Both Seymour and Sellers' stories are adapted from http://astral-institute.com/famous-people-near-death-experiences/. Additional stories are included there of Ernest Hemingway and George Lucas.

Unique features of my NDE

My first NDE was unique in several ways. First, my spirit was ushered away by an ancestor of mine. His relationship with me seemed more like a guardian angel, or according to Hawaiian culture, an 'aumakua who serves as a family protector. The second difference is I was taken to a small room, like a waiting room, that kept me away from contacting any other spirits. This small room restricted my movement, and I was not allowed beyond its walls. Third, although I was kept separate from the other spirits in this realm, I could see whom they represented. The final difference was having a conversation about the meaning of my name, Imaikalani.

Where does the name Imaikalani come from?

The name Imaikalani has its roots in ancient Hawaii. Imaikalani was a highly skilled warrior who was blinded during battle. He retired to the forest to recuperate from his wounds. Imaikalani's enemies saw this as their opportunity to finally vanquish their foe, so they hunted him down. Knowing Imaikalani's enemies were out to destroy him, his gods sent him a pair of Koloa ducks to help him. Imaikalani understood the meaning behind all the sounds the quacking ducks made. When his enemies approached his camp, the ducks flew into the air and circled above. From their vantage point, the ducks could see how many warriors Imaikalani faced, from what direction they were approaching, as well as the type of weapon each of them was armed with. The ducks became Imaikalani's eyes in the sky and would signal all the information regarding the approaching enemy to him. As the warriors attacked, the ducks would call out their movements and Imaikalani would successfully counter each move and swiftly dispatch each of his enemies. This partnership highlights the importance of trust between the messengers and the receiver. Imaikalani had to trust that the messages he heard were true and he had to exercise faith to act correctly when he received those messages.

Summary

Near-death experiences are common human events. In this chapter, you learned the definition of an NDE along with its common characteristics. You were then given historical examples of people who experienced NDEs, followed by an account of my first NDE.

Exercise

Think about a time when you were extremely ill or experienced a traumatic physical or emotional event. Did you have a strange dream or vision during this time? If so, describe the details of this dream or vision in the space below:

_____

_____

_____

_____

_____

_____

_____

_____

_____

_____

_____

How did this dream or vision affect your condition at the time?

_____

_____

_____

_____

_____

What does your name mean?

_____

_____

_____

_____

_____

How have the meanings or intentions of your name influenced your life so far?

_____

_____

_____

_____

CHAPTER 2

SEEING SPIRITS AND HIDDEN OBJECTS

> "Some people can't see the color red. That doesn't mean it isn't there," she replied."
>
> — Sue Grafton, *M Is for Malice*

In the first chapter, we examined the nature of NDEs, and I described NDEs experienced by me and a few historical figures. We then looked at the unique aspects of my personal NDE. In this chapter, we will look at how my life was impacted by my first NDE. The most significant development following my first NDE dealt with my vision. I could see spirits and I developed X-ray vision.

How can head trauma affect your life?

What happens to your brain when it is traumatized? One side effect researchers have discovered is that many people who suffer head trauma soon develop psychic abilities. The area of the brain most associated with developing these abilities is the right temporal lobe.

Shawn Lerwill is one person who developed psychic abilities after suffering trauma to this area of his head. Lerwill was on a skiing trip to Utah when a skiing accident left him with a traumatic brain injury to his right temporal lobe. Over time, Lerwill's perception of the world around him began to change. While certain parts of his life became more chaotic due to loss of memory and a distorted sense of time, he began to display some incredible psychic abilities.

David Morehouse is another person who developed psychic abilities after suffering a brain injury. In 1987, Morehouse was a Ranger Company Commander, training Jordanian rangers. He was accidentally shot in the head by a machine gun round. Luckily, he was wearing a helmet, but the impact from the gunshot was damaging. While recovering, Morehouse noticed that his perceptions had changed. Eventually, he developed his psychic abilities to the point where he was recruited to participate in project Stargate, the CIA's remote viewing program. Today, David Morehouse is a very reputable remote viewing instructor, lecturer, and author. His book, *Psychic Warrior*, is one of my favorite books on remote viewing.

How did my injury affect me?

The injury I suffered when I fell from the car was a fractured occipital bone located on the back-right part of my head. This resulted in a severe concussion. The occipital bone protects the occipital lobe of the brain, which controls vision. Although injury to the occipital region is not normally associated with the development of psychic skills, new psychic abilities began to appear in me following my accident.

While recovering from the accident that led to my first NDE, I was placed in the children's ward of Shingles Hospital, located in Ho'olehua, a couple of miles from my home. The children's ward was an extra-large room with about eight beds. Most of the beds were filled when I was admitted. A couple of the children were so sick that they were placed under protective tents and constantly monitored by the ward nurses.

Healing angels

My second night in the hospital, I witnessed something amazing. The nurses completed the last round of medications and vitals around 9 p.m. Once the lights were turned off and silence ensued, we were finally able to settle down to sleep.

I was an exceptionally light sleeper and woke up every time a nurse entered the room. Just after the 2 a.m. nurse check, I tried drifting back to sleep when I felt the presence of someone in the room. I raised my head to check who it was, but I could not see anyone. My attention was immediately drawn to the ceiling above me as it began to bounce and shake like a bowl of Jell-O. I thought we were having an earthquake!

Suddenly, a large portion of the ceiling disappeared, revealing the stars and night sky. A bright shaft of light shined down through the ceiling's opening. Within the shaft of light, human shapes emerged. One by one, they descended gently into our hospital room. As these human shapes entered the room, I could see they were men and women dressed in white. I knew they were not normal human beings. Recalling how Kupuna taught me to see the true nature of beings, I decided to see if it would work in the real world. I closed my eyes and immediately saw a rainbow of lights and colors encasing each of these beings. They were not demons. These were angels sent by God. They were the good guys.

The angels surrounded the extremely ill children enclosed in the protective tents. Reaching their hands through the tents, they touched the children, stroking their heads and bodies. Other angels walked through the room and surrounded each of the remaining children's beds, touching them in the same manner. When they came to me, I closed my eyes and allowed them to do whatever they came to do. As the angels began their ministrations, I felt a powerful surge of love flowing through my body, and with it, a sense of peace that everything would be okay.

When the angels completed their task, they departed the same way they had arrived. All the other children in the ward fell into a deep sleep, snoring like drunken sailors. I also eventually fell asleep, despite my excitement to share what I had seen with anyone willing to listen.

The following morning, I reported the incident to my nurse and doctor. They concluded that I was hallucinating and dismissed what I had seen since hallucinations can occur after a severe brain injury. When my parents arrived to visit me, the doctors and nurses had already convinced them that I was seeing things that were not there. I shared the experience with my parents who listened patiently, but I knew they did not believe me.

The only people who did believe me were the children in the ward who suddenly felt better following the angelic visitation. The children with the most severe illnesses experienced a rapid recovery. Their fevers broke that morning, and in two days, they were released from the hospital. The pace of my own healing accelerated as my bones mended and some of the concussion symptoms disappeared.

Naughty spirits

As I approached the end of my hospital stay, I started noticing other strange things happening in our room. Toys and stuffed animals gifted to other children in the ward began to move around on their own late at night. These toys would fall on to the floor, then take short hops across the floor. I decided to put my new skill to the test and closed my eyes to see what was causing the stuffed animals to behave so strangely. Using my mind's eye, I saw the spirits of four children, ranging from about five to ten years old, playing with the stuffed animals on the floor. Although I had my eyes closed, they realized I could see them. These little spirits rushed to my bedside. By the time I opened my eyes, my bed was surrounded by six spirit children, eager to play with me. They were starved for attention, desperate to make human contact. They tried to talk to me, but I could not hear them. We could only communicate through hand gestures. Eventually, I learned to communicate with them telepathically, using pictures.

When morning arrived, eight spirit children were playing around my bed. Each tried desperately to monopolize my attention. I began to wonder where they had come from. I discovered their origins a couple of days later when I was wheeled into the hospital lab for some blood work and vision testing. As I entered the lab, I noticed eight large brown glass jars in neat rows on a shelf. Each jar contained a human fetus in a different stage of development.

Sadness overcame me as I realized the tiny bodies in the glass jars were the homes of the spirits visiting with me. This discovery made me more tolerant and understanding of these mischievous little spirits. Since I caught every virus and germ that hit the island as a child, I spent a lot of time in the hospital, and these little ones were always there waiting to play with me.

How was my life affected after I recovered from my injuries?

After being discharged from the hospital, I grew to understand we are surrounded by spirits, whether we invite them or not. I could feel their presence everywhere I went, and within a couple of years, I no longer needed to close my eyes to see them. Spirits are part of the environment, attracted to the same places the living are attracted to. They dot the beaches, sit in theaters, read books in school, and attend church.

The scariest experiences for me as a child were visiting friends or relatives in hospitals and attending funeral services. Hospitals and funerals attract spirits who are disoriented and confused. Many of the spirits who appeared there did not realize they were dead. Many were mournful or angry.

Growing up on Molokai, I could also see where the Lapu lapu kolohe (ghosts) hung out and found ways to avoid them. The lapu are different from the Huaka'i, or Night Marchers. The lapu are normally a lone spirit or a small group of spirits who love to scare people. They know they are dead and want to take their frustrations out on the living. They will try to lure you into situations that may hurt you, like enticing you to walk off a cliff, or run into the path of an oncoming car. Once, while I was donning a cape like my hero Superman, a lapu convinced me I could fly. I climbed to the rooftop of our house and tried to soar with the birds. Fortunately, my ancestors were watching, and I landed harmlessly into our hibiscus bush. The only thing bruised was my ego.

The Huaka'i consist of a large group of spirits who keep reliving a specific event trapped in time. They march the same trail, follow the same patterns, and have no intentions of scaring anyone. Their paths are well known to many native families.

A trail used by the Huaka'i cut right through our Ho'olehua Homestead. This group of Night Marchers were athletes traveling to and from the Na'iwa Makahiki grounds located in a valley just northwest of our homestead. During the Makahiki season (the ancient Hawaiian New Year festival), which ran from late December until the middle of January, Huaka'i would march past our home, carrying their spears, baskets of food, and the supplies they needed to compete at the games held at Na'iwa. Our howling dogs would signal their arrival and departure.

Have other people seen angels or spirits?

I have many gifted family members who could see and communicate with spirits. Here are a few examples of their experiences.

Captain David Kenison

One of my favorite family stories of ghostly encounters involves my great-great-grandfather, Captain David Kenison. Captain Kenison owned a shipping company that shipped goods between Samoa, New Zealand, and Australia. The Southern Ocean is one of the most treacherous seas to navigate. Captain Kenison was a master at navigating these waters.

During one of his trips, Captain Kenison ran into a major storm that caused him to become disoriented. His charts and compass could not help him, and the skies were too cloudy for him to navigate by the stars. As his options slowly disappeared, Captain Kenison prayed for divine guidance. A short time later, in the middle of this great storm, something strange appeared off his ship's bow. It was white and glowing in the darkness. Upon closer observation, this glowing object appeared to be a woman's arm. Captain Kenison soon realized the arm was that of his wife Elizabeth. Elizabeth's arm began to point out the direction Captain Kenison should steer his ship. Acting on faith, Captain Kenison steered his ship according to his wife's directions. Captain Kenison was able to navigate safely through the storm and arrived with his ship and cargo intact at his home port of Pago Pago. When he docked his ship, his family members gave him the sad news. His wife Elizabeth had died. Elizabeth's spirit had helped her husband find his way home.

Gigi

I had an unusual incident with my daughter Gigi when she was about four years old. We were living in a pastor's cottage on the grounds of the Hoʻolehua Congregational Church. Some of the parishioners had negative feelings about me living in the pastor's cottage since I was a Mormon and did not attend their church. Sometimes, these kinds of negative feelings can create their own entity.

Gigi and I had just gotten home from shopping when I opened the door to our home and stepped inside. Gigi remained frozen on the porch, holding tightly to her package. Her eyes were fixed toward the ceiling inside to our left. I asked Gigi, "What's wrong, my girl? You see something?"

Gigi nodded "yes" and pointed to the top left corner of the room.

"Bad man!"

"What is the bad man doing?"

Gigi opened her mouth, exposing her teeth, and made a mean-looking face.

I looked toward the same corner Gigi was fixated on and saw a shadow-like figure. I summoned God and my ancestors to drive this entity away from my home. The shadow moved along the edge of the ceiling until it was above our door. I grabbed hold of Gigi's hand and stepped inside the home. The entity left the house through the back door.

Did my ability to see spirits lead to new abilities?

As my spiritual vision sharpened, I soon discovered I could see more than just spirits. I learned that despite objects being hidden away, locked in a desk, or sitting in a purse, I could see and describe them quite accurately just by focusing my attention there.

Christmas and birthday parties

A trigger event that pushed me into intentionally seeing hidden objects occurred one Christmas morning following my eighth birthday when we started opening our presents. When I grabbed one of my presents, one of my sisters teased me and said that the gift was

"BBDs," our term for underwear. I hated being teased, so I used all my focus to look deeply into the wrapped gift. I saw the colors blue, white, and red, and then noticed it was a striped cloth. I then saw buttons and a collar. The object wrapped inside my present was a striped shirt. I looked at my sister and told her, "It's a shirt, not BBDs."

I unwrapped the gift, and it was indeed a striped shirt! I tossed my shirt to my sister, and said, "See, it's a shirt, not BBDs." She had a puzzled look on her face as she examined the shirt. I knew she was thinking, *How the hell did he do that?* She then scowled and tossed the shirt back to me, muttering "Weirdo" beneath her breath. I laughed since I had discovered a new way to irritate my sister.

Encouraged by my success in seeing my shirt, I then looked at the rest of my unopened gifts and began to sort them into different stacks. Clothes went in one stack, books and school supplies in another, and finally there was a stack for my toys. I then opened my gifts, beginning with my clothes (the boring stuff), followed by my books and school supplies, and then the toys, saving the best for last. This became a habitual practice at every Christmas or birthday party whenever I received gifts.

Taking my gift beyond our home

The first time I recall using my ability to see hidden objects outside the home was at a birthday party for a friend. We were both ten years old. Everyone at the party was sitting around the birthday girl as she opened her presents. Just as my friend was about to unwrap a gift, one of the boys yelled out:

"Panties! Panties!"

Several of the other children laughed, but I felt bad for my friend. She sat there with the gift in her hands, too embarrassed to open it. I turned my attention to the wrapped gift. I saw something red and fluffy like wool, warm and woven like a sweater.

I looked at my friend and reassured her, "Don't worry; it's not panties. It's a red wool sweater, probably something your mom made for you."

She cautiously opened the gift. It was indeed a red and white wool sweater handmade by her mom.

She picked up another gift and asked if I could guess what was inside that one too. Being an avid reader, I saw the gift was the same size as a book. I closed my eyes and saw a picture of a girl on the cover. My guess: A Nancy Drew book. The gift was unwrapped, and it was a Nancy Drew book. I went on to accurately describe eight of the ten gifts that day.

Displaying my ability at this party affected my relationship with my peers. I was now the weirdo most kids were afraid to hang out with. It never occurred to me that no one else could see spirits or hidden objects. I thought everyone had this ability. My peers only acknowledged me when they wanted to hear a spooky story. Otherwise, I was a pariah. I became the loner introvert with only a handful of loyal friends.

Despite being shunned for my abilities, I continued to exercise my ability to see hidden objects at birthday parties for my friends and family members. As the celebrants prepared to open their gifts, I would sneak a peek to identify the gift inside. I got to be annoyingly accurate, upsetting a lot of people in the process. I eventually learned that because I could see and sense things very well, it was better to keep my observations to myself. Nobody likes a know-it-all. Eventually, I went silent and would not share the things I saw or felt beyond my closest friends and family members.

Realizing the nature of my sacred name

My first important soul journey occurred when I was five. As my ability to see and communicate with spirits strengthened, everything Kupuna had told me about my name was coming true. I was able to see spirits and recognize the difference between angels and other spirit forms. I could converse with my ancestors and began to develop a working relationship with them. I could also see things people were hiding from me. I learned to trust what I saw and had the confidence to share, but I also used wisdom in sharing what I saw with other people.

Summary

In this chapter, we examined the effect of a head injury on the development of psychic abilities. Although my injury was to the back of my head, I began to see spirits and hidden objects. Seeing spirits everywhere was frightening at times, but I learned to deal with that over time. I also developed the ability to see hidden objects. My accident and NDE helped define me according to my sacred name.

Exercise

If you had the ability to see spirits or hidden objects, how would you use this ability?

_____

_____

_____

_____

_____

_____

_____

What guidelines would you recommend to people who have this gift?

_____

_____

_____

_____

_____

_____

_____

_____

_____

CHAPTER 3
CLASHING OF CULTURES

> "It is in middles that extremes clash, where
> ambiguity restlessly rules."
>
> — John Updike

In the last chapter, we examined my ability to see spirits and hidden objects that followed my first NDE and accident. In this chapter, I will examine the problems that arose from my newfound abilities that began to show themselves in my home, school, and church.

How does the influence of multiple cultures impact a gifted child?

For a gifted child, the presence of multiple cultures that often compete and conflict with each other can be very frustrating and confusing. What may be perfectly acceptable in one culture may be forbidden in another. I faced this situation as a child as I tried to find a balance between three dominating cultures within our island community: the Hawaiian, Mormon, and Plantation cultures.

Hawaiian Culture

I was born and raised in the Hawaiian community of Hoʻolehua, Molokai. Our community was established by the Hawaiian Homes Commission Act of 1921, which set aside public lands for homesteading. Native Hawaiians were given the opportunity to return to the land and become self-sufficient homesteaders.

When the first homesteaders arrived in Hoʻolehua, they faced a huge obstacle: Hoʻolehua was a desert, with hardly any rainfall. For Molokai natives, the reason for the lack of rain was the *Imu Kalua Ua* (the oven to roast the rain). This small, rectangular stone labyrinth, covering about twenty square feet, was built in ancient times to trap and kill the rain god, a goal that was successful. Without rain, farming the Hoʻolehua plains would be nearly impossible. Another challenge facing the early homesteaders were the Lapu lapu kolohe, or rascal spirits/ghosts, who had claimed much of the land as theirs. As humans encroached upon their domains, the lapu fought back with hauntings and illnesses.

During ancient times, the Molokai natives were famous for their spiritual powers. Molokai was referred to as *Molokai Pule Oʻo*, or Molokai, where the prayers bear fruit. The people did not need a standing army to defend themselves. One story tells of an invading chief from Maui, who, when approaching Molokai, was held offshore by an invisible force that did not allow the canoes to approach the shore. Molokai became the training grounds for Kahuna and ceremonial temple arts. The power of the ancients could still be felt in the land.

The dark art of ʻAnaʻana has part of its roots on Molokai. These roots are found near the village of Maunaloa on the west side of Molokai. A grove of sacred trees once grew near Maunaloa, which was a gift from the gods to a gambler. When people discovered this grove, they tried to harvest some of the trees. While cutting down a tree, pieces of the tree struck a bystander, who died instantly. More trees were later harvested and carved into what were called the Kalae Pahoa gods, or poison gods, who could be used to pray people to death. Kamehameha the Great possessed one of these gods that is now on display at the Bishop Museum in Honolulu.

This is the type of mana, or living energy, that existed throughout this land.

My paternal grandmother, Ellen, was a gifted healer and interpreter of dreams. As a healer, grandma used her knowledge of herbs, energy, and prayer to heal others from illnesses that could be physical, emotional, mental, or spiritual. She used the process of Hoʻoponopono to resolve conflicts among groups of people. Grandma understood the symbolic nature of dreams and helped people understand their nightmares.

Grandma had a strong connection to her ancestors and our ʻaumakua or family guardian, Pukonanui. Pukonanui was our ancestor from Tahiti. He was also a demigod. On land, he was a tall, slender man, but when he entered the ocean, he transformed into a great eel. Pukonanui saved our family from annihilation by transporting his two sisters on his back from Tahiti until he reached Maui. For this reason, Pukonanui was made our family guardian, and the eel, or puhi, became a sacred entity to our family. We were taught to respect the eel and not eat it.

Grandma Ellen did not see any conflict in showing respect to the older Hawaiian gods and ʻaumakua while being a Mormon. She saw more things uniting these beliefs than making them different. Because of her beliefs and practices, many people in our community and family called grandma a kahuna, a term often associated with those who practice the dark arts.

Mormon culture

When the Hawaiian Homes Commission decided to open Hoʻolehua for settlement, they recruited farmers who made their living in lands like Hoʻolehua. They found many of these early recruits in Kula, Maui. Several of these early settlers were my family members, the Makaiwi and Wallace families.

My family members arrived in Hoʻolehua to take on the challenge of settling the land and making it productive. They realized that to make the land green again, they needed water. After meeting as a family, they decided to use their Mormon faith and practices to ask God to return the rains to Hoʻolehua. The family exercised their faith by fasting and praying for rain.

I recall my uncle Kuamu Pelekai telling the story of how the rains returned. Kuamu was a young man when this fast was called. After several days of prayer, fasting, and going hungry, he went outside of the house and looked up into the sky. There was nothing but blue sky. Disappointed, he sat down and began chatting with his cousins. After a few minutes, he looked back up into the sky and noticed a small, puffy white cloud all by itself. It was not impressive, just a tiny speck of white in the vast blue sky. As he watched the cloud, it began to grow larger and larger. Within a few minutes, this tiny little cloud filled the entire sky! By then, the entire family was in the yard, looking at this wonderful cloud getting thicker and darker until, finally, rain began to fall. This rain lasted for several days, quenching the thirst of the land, and watering the crops. After that incident, the rains returned to the Hoʻolehua plains on a regular basis. My family were able to plant and harvest their crops, which opened the Hoʻolehua area for permanent settlement. The curse of the Imu Kalua Ua was broken.

Spirits

Multiple levels of spiritual problems existed on Molokai when my family tried to settle the area in the 1930s. My family members were transplants from Maui, so they did not have a history or connection to Molokai. Sometimes, ignorance has its upside.

The roving mischievous spirits known as the Lapu lapu kolohe can create a lot of problems for people who encroach on their territories. Since Hoʻolehua was vacant of humans for hundreds of years, the lands were claimed by the lapu. As the early settlers began to establish their homesteads on the land, they ran into conflicts with the lapu. Even when I was a child growing up on Molokai during the 1950s, hauntings, possessions, and poltergeists were quite common. To combat the lapu, my family again turned to their priesthood and used it to clear homes, cast out demons, and cleanse the land. The Mormon priesthood's early success in restoring water to the land and combatting the lapu firmly established the Mormon Church in Ho'olehua.

Mom

My mom, Maggie, was born in 1929 in Laie, Oahu, a community owned and developed by the Mormon Church. Mom's family were early converts to the Mormon faith. Mom's father and grandfather, John and Charles Broad, had migrated to Salt Lake City, Utah, so they could do temple work for their ancestors. Temple work involved performing baptisms and temple ordinances by proxy on behalf of your deceased family members. John and Charles became part of the Iosepa Colony in Skull Valley, located in Tooele County, Utah. This colony was established by the Mormon Church to care for the displaced Polynesians who found themselves in a strange land with strange customs. When the Church acquired large tracts of land in Laie, Oahu, and planned to build a temple there, many of the Polynesians living in Iosepa were convinced to move to Laie to help build the temple. My grandparents, with two young sons, Edwin and Lionel, moved back to Hawaii and settled in Laie.

The Laie community had its own issues with syncretism; stories of possessions, hauntings, and people holding on to old Hawaiian customs were part of Laie in its early days. Despite that, the Mormon Church and its leaders dominated Laie. For my mom and her family, the Mormon Church became the center of their lives. Grandma and Grandpa Broad were continually active members of the Church. This strongly influenced my mom's life and belief system.

Syncretism

Despite the Mormon Church's early success in Hoʻolehua, many families chose to cling to traditional Hawaiian practices. For many of these families, no difference existed between the concept of Father, Son, and Holy Ghost taught in most Christian faiths and the concept of Ku, Kane, and Lono, the main gods worshiped by our ancestors. Many Hawaiians accepted both belief systems as true.

The old Hawaiian practices were alive and functioning when I was a child, as evidenced by watching the night sky. Sometimes, we would see fiery airborne objects, known as *akualele*, slowly gliding past our home heading east or west. Akualele resembled shooting stars, with a round glowing head and a long bright tail. They were not meteors, but spirits summoned to do evil deeds. Akualele were normally controlled by a person who had enslaved a spirit. The master would use this spirit to cause illness or even death to another person. To send the enslaved spirit to its intended victim, the master would weave a ball and command the spirit to occupy the ball. When the spirit entered the ball, it would give off a glow and appear to be on fire. This ball of fire would then be sent to the victim. While traveling to the intended victim, the akualele will fly and appear to be a fireball in the sky, visible to everyone. When the ball reached its victim, the ball would explode, releasing the spirit, which would then possess the victim. Seeing red, green, and blue akualele was quite a common sight for us when I was a child. The color of the akualele and the direction it originated from was often enough for us to know who had sent it.

Syncretism is still alive in Hawaii today. For example, a Christian priest will give a blessing over a new business, then dip a ti leaf in a bowl of salt water and sprinkle the salt water onto the doorway to bless the building. When I was a child on Molokai, it was sometimes difficult to distinguish between Hawaiian culture and my Mormon culture.

Plantation culture

Molokai's primary employers during my childhood were the pineapple companies Del Monte and Libby's. Del Monte was based out of Kualapu'u, about a mile east from our homestead. Libby's had its main base in Maunaloa on the west end of Molokai, but it had another base yard in Ho'olehua for its workers who lived in the central and eastern parts of the island.

Both companies and the communities that surrounded them followed a similar plantation organization. The big bosses and managers for these plantations were Haole (Caucasians) with a few Japanese or Chinese men placed in top management roles. Japanese, Filipinos, and Hawaiians made up the bulk of the manual laborers, truck drivers, and machine operators. The gang foremen or *luna* were normally chosen from the same ethnicity as the gang of workers.

The disparity in the plantation system could be seen just by looking at the workers' housing. The plantation housing was divided along ethnic lines. The larger homes with large open yards belonged to the Haole bosses. Japanese camps had smaller homes than the Haoles, but their homes were larger than the ones given to other ethnicities. The smallest housing units, which were crowded like toy blocks, went to the Filipinos, Hawaiians, and any other ethnic minorities. Each camp maintained its social distance from the others and the residents kept to themselves as much as possible.

Preferential treatment of different races carried over from the plantations into our schools. Haoles and Japanese (as well as other Asians) were expected to succeed and were often placed in different classes than Filipinos and Hawaiians. The teachers were either Haole or Asian and perpetuated the same values as the plantations. Haole and Asian kids were encouraged to excel while Hawaiians were told they were lazy and only good for manual labor. I will never forget the reaction of my Haole eighth grade science teacher when I told him I wanted to go to college. He sneered at me and said, "You'll never make it!"

Mom meets the dark side of Molokai

After my mom and dad got married on December 27, 1947, Mom moved to Molokai to live with my dad. Their first home on my grandmother's homestead was a makeshift shack with a dirt floor and no running water. An outhouse was built next to the shack to accommodate their needs. Trouble developed when mom got pregnant with my brother Bill, her firstborn.

Many Hawaiian and Polynesian families practice the concept of *hanai* (adopting children). Grandparents would hanai a few of the grandchildren or infants from close relatives and raise them as their own. This way, when the grandparents were old, they would have someone young and strong to care for them. Following this tradition, Grandma Ellen approached my mom, pointed at her stomach, and said:

"That baby is mine."

Mom coolly replied, "My momma told me if I could not take care of my baby, she would help me raise my child."

Mom would not give in. Several nights later, Mom had a strange dream.

In the dream, Mom woke up to use the outhouse. As she walked out of the shack, she was confronted by an akualele. It appeared as a glowing ball of white light about the size of a basketball that had a long, skinny, wiggly tail, like a balloon with a thick string attached to it. The akualele aligned itself with my mom's stomach. As my mom moved, the akualele followed her stomach. Realizing the akualele was after her child, Mom knelt on the pathway and said a prayer, calling on God to help her. In an instant, her father, John, appeared.

"What's the matter, girlie?" asked Grandpa John.

"Papa, there's an akualele trying to take my baby!"

Grandpa John hugged Mom and comforted her.

"Don't you worry. I'll take care of it."

As soon as Grandpa John spoke those words, the akualele dove into the bushes to hide. Grandpa John tracked it down and grabbed it by its tail. The akualele squirmed and fought like a landed fish, but it could not escape Grandpa's firm grip. Grandpa opened the door to the outhouse and threw the akualele down into the dung heap. He dropped his pants and took a major poop right on the akualele. The akualele exploded, releasing the enslaved spirit, which immediately fled the area. According to tradition, an akualele that fails to possess its victim will return to the person who sent it, making the person ill.

The morning after this dream, Mom went over to Grandma Ellen's house and learned Grandma Ellen was terribly ill. Mom then realized who was responsible for the dream. From that point on, Mom and Grandma Ellen never got along.

Caught in the middle

From the time I was little, I always loved to visit Grandma Ellen and Grandpa William, my dad's parents, on their homestead on Farrington Avenue. Grandpa loved to plant a wide variety of crops, including peanuts, sweet potatoes, bananas, and corn. Sometimes, he grew watermelons. My grandparents always had chickens with chicks running around the yard.

Every time we pulled up to their driveway and saw other cars at the house, we would hear cabinets slamming and people running around inside the kitchen. When we kissed our grandparents or visiting family, we understood what the slamming doors meant. We could smell cigarettes and alcohol on their breaths, something Mormons should not be doing. As kids, we really did not care what they were doing; that was their business.

Every time I had alone time with my grandma, she would rub my head and tell me, "Remember, you good boy, okay?"

As my gifts of seeing spirits and hidden objects began to display themselves, I wanted to spend more time with Grandma Ellen to see if she could help me understand my gifts better. I knew she was a healer and had the vision to perceive things very well. Once my mom caught wind of that, she tried everything in her power to cut me and the rest of our family off from Grandma Ellen.

How did these cultural, family, and community values affect me as a child?

An interesting perception I learned from listening to my grandpa John was how he and his generation valued their European ancestry and heritage more than their Hawaiian identities. When Grandpa John spoke of his ethnicity, he would list his family as Irish, Scottish, English, French, and some Hawaiian. This from a man who was three-fourths Hawaiian!

During Grandpa John's childhood, the schools prohibited Hawaiians from speaking their native language. Hawaiian children were punished if they were caught speaking it. By the time I entered school, none of my peers spoke Hawaiian. We did not even know how to swear in Hawaiian! It took just a few generations to strip Hawaiians of their language and culture and supplant it with American and Western language and culture. Anything Hawaiian was viewed as having a lesser value than anything American or European.

The plantation mentality was reinforced in school by teachers who were Haole or Asian. The Haole and Asian students were normally given positions of authority or trust while Hawaiians and Filipinos were delegated to menial roles in school. Hawaiians were called lazy, and not expected to accomplish much. We were reminded almost every day of our shortcomings. My saving grace as a Hawaiian was having the last name Wallace.

As I grew older and my abilities became stronger, I instinctively knew Grandma Ellen could help me. Mom was convinced Grandma Ellen was a kahuna, and she did not want me or any of my siblings to be part of that. To deal with my growing awareness, she turned to the Mormon Church. I remember spending many hours explaining to our branch president about the things I saw and felt. Fortunately, some of these leaders understood my dilemma, but as leaders in the Church, they could not help me. Their answer to everything was a priesthood blessing.

Eventually, I submitted to the Mormon culture and adopted beliefs and behaviors that conformed with my family and the Church. I turned away from my Hawaiian heritage and worked extremely hard to decrease the influences of my visions and dreams. I concentrated on trying to become a good Mormon American, even accepting the role of a second-class citizen. By the time I was a teenager, I had become another brainwashed Hawaiian.

Summary

In this chapter, we looked at the complex community of my childhood and how it influenced my development as a gifted child. American values and customs supported by the Mormon faith became my accepted perspective. While my gifts continued to grow and display themselves, they were frowned upon by my church. Eventually, I had to ignore everything I saw or dreamed about.

Exercise

Which cultural or religious beliefs or practices that you learned as a child have helped create the person you are today?

_____

_____

_____

_____

_____

_____

_____

_____

_____

_____

CHAPTER 4

DREAMING AND PROPHECY

"Dream lofty dreams, and as you dream, so you shall become. Your vision is the promise of what you shall one day be; your ideal is the prophecy of what you shall at last unveil."

— James Allen

In the previous chapter, we discussed the conflict that existed between the Hawaiian, Mormon, and Plantation cultures in the community I grew up in. For a gifted child, this conflict led to many internal struggles as I tried to make sense of my life. In this chapter, we will examine an especially important ability that began to fully display itself as I grew into adulthood: my ability to have prophetic dreams.

What are prophetic dreams?

Have you ever had disturbing dreams that eventually came true? Have you ever tried warning people about what you saw in these dreams? What were their reactions? If you have ever done this, then you understand the dilemma many prophetic dreamers like me face. People think you are crazy.

Prophetic dreams are dreams that reveal things that eventually occur in real life. Some people's prophetic dreams will reveal themselves within a few days of the dream, while others have dreams that do not materialize until several years later. Most of my prophetic dreams come true within three days, while some dreams take much longer to materialize. I had one series of prophetic dreams that took more than forty years to manifest.

Dreams play a vital role in many native cultures and are taken very seriously. They are an important tool for the *kahuna kaula* (seer) in Hawaiian culture. From our own family traditions, we are reminded to pay attention to our dreams just before waking and dreams that repeat themselves at least three times.

Several important figures throughout history have received prophetic dreams. Here are two examples.

Famous prophetic dreams

Three days prior to his assassination, Abraham Lincoln related a prophetic dream he had to his wife and a few friends foreshadowing his death.

In his dream, President Lincoln encountered "the subdued sobs of mourners." Walking from room to room, he noticed a corpse lying on a catafalque in the White House East Room. In the dream, Lincoln asked a soldier standing guard, "Who is dead in the White House?" The soldier replied, "The President. He was killed by an assassin."

Lincoln jumped out of bed at that point on April 11. Three days after his vivid nightmare, Lincoln was shot dead at point blank range by assassin John Wilkes Booth while attending the theater.

Not all dreams are of pending doom. One dream led to the invention of the sewing machine. Elias Howe invented the sewing machine in 1845. He had the idea of a machine with a needle that would go through a piece of cloth, but he could not figure out exactly how it would work. In a dream, Howe found himself in an awkward situation. Cannibals were preparing to cook him, and they were dancing around the fire waving their spears. Howe noticed at the head of each spear was a small hole through the shaft. The up-and-down motion of the spears and the hole at the tip of the spear remained with him when he woke. The idea of passing the thread through the needle close to the point, not at the other end, was a major innovation in making mechanical sewing possible.

Family prophecies

One intriguing family story associated with prophecy concerns my great-great-grandfather John Henry Broad who lived in Kona, located on the west coast of Hawaii Island. John was a wealthy landowner who lived near the ocean, but he also had farmlands in the cool uplands, as was common for landowners on Kona. Since Kona was hot during the day, farmers would wait until early in the morning before the sun rose to travel to their farmlands.

Several hours after midnight, John would load up his gear onto his horse, then ride the trail to his upland farm. At one point along the trail, a spirit would appear and keep John company until he reached his farm plot. This went on for several years, and John and this spirit developed a fond relationship.

One night, John must have been in a very sour mood because when the spirit approached him at the usual spot, John turned nasty and began to verbally abuse it. Upset that John would turn on him, the spirit told him that when he died, the pigs in the forest would be better off, since the pigs have fur to cover their bodies. The spirit declared that when John died, he would be stripped naked and dumped into a hole. That was the last John ever heard from this spirit.

Several years later, John became one of the casualties of a cholera epidemic that hit the Big Island. To make sure the disease did not spread, all his clothes were taken and burned. John was stripped naked, wrapped in a sheet, and lowered to his grave. The prophecy of the spirit was fulfilled.

My prophetic dreams

Chaz

One of my prophetic dreams involved Chaz, a friend from Molokai. During my short career as a firefighter, Chaz and I worked in the same firehouse and became good friends. Realizing our appointments as firefighters were only temporary, we both took and passed the police test for the County of Maui. We were hired by the Maui Police Department in 1977.

Chaz and I moved to Maui in the summer of 1977 and were immediately placed to work at the central police station in Wailuku until recruit school started. Just before our recruit class began, I received a disturbing dream that repeated itself for three consecutive nights.

In my dream, I was standing outside a large building with a group of uniformed police officers. I saw some of my fellow recruits dressed in brand new police uniforms and dark glasses with reflective lenses. We were wearing our badges, Sam Brown belts, side arms, speed loaders, and handcuffs. As I looked at our badges, I saw a black stripe across them. I then noticed I was wearing a pair of white gloves. I realized a police officer had died.

A stern-looking sergeant approached us and created two columns of officers. I was the first person in the left wing of the formation, and my cousin Newton, another recruit from Molokai, stood to my right, leading his column. Six of us were in this unit.

The sergeant led us to the front of this large building where we stood at the base of a tall set of stairs that led to double doors opened outward. We marched up the stairs and entered the room. A red cross made of flowers was on the front wall. Next to the cross was a wall clock that had been stopped at 1:35. The room was filled with rows of people dressed in black and white. The mood was very somber.

The building looked like a church, but it did not feel like a church. We marched down the aisle. When we came to the front of the room, the sergeant stopped us from advancing and told Newton and me to "post."

Newton and I turned to our right. I then noticed a gray casket to our right with the lid closed. Newton walked past the casket, and I stood near the part of the casket where the head of the person would be.

Going into parade rest, I stood next to the casket, wondering who was inside. Just as a man began a prayer to start the service, I heard someone snoring inside the casket. I looked at the people in the audience; everyone's eyes were closed in prayer. I glanced at the casket, and to my horror, the lid popped open! The snoring got even louder. I panicked and reached over to close the casket lid. I glanced down into the casket and saw that the snoring man was Chaz.

I leaned over into the casket and whispered to Chaz, trying to be as discreet as possible, "Chaz, what the hell you doing sleeping in there? Get up and get out of there, man!"

Chaz yawned and stretched his hands, then opened his eyes.

"Eh, David John, what's up?"

"What's up? You crazy buggah, what are you doing sleeping in this casket?"

"I was sleeping and woke up inside here. Go figure." Chaz chuckled in amusement.

"You think that's funny? Come on; let me help you out."

I reached inside the casket to pull Chaz out, but he grabbed me by my collar and pulled me to within an inch of his face. I then noticed a large wound in the center of his forehead.

"David John," he said soberly, "don't worry about me. Tell my sons I love them."

Chaz pushed me away, and the lid to the casket slammed shut. I rushed to the casket and tried to pry Chaz out. The man saying the prayer ended, and when everyone opened their eyes, I was found hugging the casket, crying. My dream ended there.

I tried to dismiss the dream as a weird fantasy. But after having the same dream the next two nights, I knew Chaz was in danger.

We were working different shifts at the time, and for some reason, I could not contact Chaz. I kept missing him at shift change. I asked his sergeant to have Chaz meet me somewhere so we could talk. I learned Chaz was working his shift, then going straight to Kihei to play softball. Chaz's plate was very full, so he did not have the time to meet with me. I decided to let things settle down for Chaz; then we could have our talk. Unfortunately, time ran out for Chaz.

About a week after receiving these dreams, I had just completed working the first watch, from 10 p.m. to 7 a.m. I went home to my apartment, ate breakfast, showered, and went to bed. Just after noon, I heard the phone ringing. I normally let my roommates answer the phone while I was sleeping, but for some reason, I sprang from my bed and picked up the phone. On the other end was a police dispatcher. She informed me I needed to go to Maui Memorial's emergency room because Chaz had been in a motor vehicle accident. A feeling of dread overcame me.

"Is Chaz okay?"

"Check with the sergeant when you get there, okay?"

I knew that meant things were not going well for Chaz.

I threw on some clothes and sped to the hospital. When I got there, several officers and some of Chaz's friends were outside the OR where the doctors were attempting to save Chaz's life. A sense of gloom and despair filled everyone's eyes.

Since I was the closest person to family Chaz had, the doctor allowed me to enter the OR. I saw Chaz's injuries. They were profoundly serious. His breathing was labored. Within ten minutes of my entering the OR, the doctor in charge declared that Chaz's eyes were dilated and fixed.

"Time of death," called out the doctor as he glanced at the clock on the wall, "1:35 p.m."

My heart sank to the floor. I said my goodbyes to Chaz and left the room sobbing.

I later learned Chaz had been driving back and forth between work in Wailuku and softball games in Kihei for several days. He was also attending post-game parties, which carried on into the wee hours of the morning. He was not getting any sleep between work, games, and partying. During his final trip, Chaz drove from Kihei along Honoapiilani Highway toward Wailuku. Somewhere between Waikapu and Wailuku, Chaz fell asleep at the wheel and collided with a monkey pod tree stump on the highway's shoulder. His death happened by a matter of inches. Had the tree stump been cut just a few inches shorter, Chaz would have had an embarrassing moment of running his car off into the cane fields. He would still be alive today.

Discovering that Chaz fell asleep at the wheel explained why I had heard the snoring in the casket. The clock on the wall in my dream had given his time of death. It was not until his wake at Bulgo's Mortuary in Wailuku that the rest of the dream made sense.

Since Chaz came from Molokai, my cousin Newton and I became part of Chaz's honor guard. The rest of the honor guard were police officers who had become Chaz's close friends, even though he had been with the department for only a few short months. The recruits who were part of the honor guard were given temporary uniforms and badges along with some dress shoes. After meeting the rest of the officers outside the mortuary, one of the sergeants met us and gave us instructions for the honor guard. Newton and I were placed in front of the honor guard, with Newton leading the right column and me leading the left.

We marched to the front of the mortuary's funeral hall where we faced a long set of stairs leading up into the hall. At the top of the stairs were double doors that opened outward. When we marched into the funeral hall, I noticed a cross made of red flowers hanging high on the room's front wall. Marching down the aisle, I looked to my right and left. I recognized some people in attendance from my dream.

Finally, we reached the front of the funeral hall and I turned right. I saw the same gray casket as in my dream. We posted at our spots, me by the head of the casket, and Newton near the foot. The casket's lid was closed.

I went into parade rest and listened to the opening remarks being made by a family representative. When a man took the podium to say the opening prayer, I began my own prayer:

"Okay, Chaz, don't you dare snore on me now!"

For the longest time after Chaz's death, I wondered if it would have made a difference if I had been more assertive about sharing the warning I had received. My guilt prompted me to take these types of dreams seriously. After I shared my warnings, people had to assume the responsibility for their own fate. That is the situation I found myself in a few years later with Corporal Mick.

Corporal Mick

I was hired as a patrol officer by the Brigham Young University Police Department in Provo, Utah, in 1982. Since I had three years of experience with the Maui Police Department, I was placed with an inexperienced yet connected officer, Corporal Mick. Besides receiving a particularly good salary and health coverage for me and my family, working for BYU had wonderful benefits. First, we had access to every door on campus, which included racquetball courts, saunas, and weight rooms. I remember playing 4-on-4 on the Marriot Center basketball court with other officers. We had the keys to the kingdom. The most important benefit to me was BYU employees could take up to six credits per semester tuition-free. This was a great opportunity to finish my schooling.

Working with Corporal Mick could be trying at times since he was extremely inexperienced and made a lot of mistakes. Despite this, we got along and developed a respectful relationship.

Early one morning, I had a remarkably interesting dream involving Corporal Mick. I knew he was a scoutmaster for his ward, so seeing him in a dream dressed in his scouting uniform was not unusual. What was unusual was he was leading his troop of young boys up the face of a steep, slick granite cliff. I watched him as he slid along a very narrow path that was wet and slippery. He managed to take the group of boys almost to the top of the trail, when suddenly, he lost his grip and fell from the mountain.

I watched as he fell with a surprised look on his face. He landed with a loud THUD.

I quickly ran to him, screaming his name.

"Mick!"

When I reached his body, Mick was no longer wearing his Boy Scout uniform. He was wearing his BYU Police uniform, with his badge and weapons on his belt. The impact of the fall blew out his internal organs as if he had exploded from the inside, revealing his heart, intestines, and ribs. His eyes and mouth were wide open, with his look of surprise and horror frozen in time.

I woke up crying from this dream. Fortunately, I was scheduled to work with Corporal Mick that very day.

When I arrived at work, I asked Corporal Mick to meet me for a private chat after we completed our initial rounds of the BYU campus. We eventually met for lunch at the BYU cafeteria. I found a place where we could chat without listening ears. I told him about my dream and warned him to stay away from high places made of granite. The dream appeared to be more symbolic than realistic, so he needed to be aware of his surroundings if he was doing something dangerous around slick granite objects. Corporal Mick assured me he would be careful, but for some reason, I felt he did not believe anything I had told him.

Less than a week later, I learned our detectives had arrested Corporal Mick for burglary. He had used his keys to enter his professor's room and was caught making copies of the professor's answer key for an upcoming test. The professor had suspected something unusual was occurring since Corporal Mick was struggling with the class but acing the exams. The professor also noticed someone had been entering his room and leaving things out of order. He contacted our detectives, who placed a silent alarm in his room. Because the suspect was a police officer, no one in the patrol division had any clue about this.

How does Corporal Mick's crime relate to my dream? The building Corporal Mick was arrested in was the Tanner Building, located on the lower BYU campus. The building is made of highly polished granite and sits at the edge of a cliff that was formed when the grounds were part of a quarry. Corporal Mick's crime exposed him for the type of person he was—a cheat and a fraud without honor. Being the nephew of one of the leaders of the LDS Church only made his dishonor worse.

Receiving prophetic dreams was an extension of my ability to see spirits and hidden objects. What made these dreams different is that they connected me to future times and allowed me to prepare myself and others to meet future challenges. Many of my prophetic dreams helped me prepare for job interviews, where I met with the people who would be interviewing me and heard their questions in my dream. This made it easier for me to find the best responses to my interviewers' questions. Other dreams dealt with my relationships with friends and relatives. When anyone would pose a danger to me or my family, they showed up in my dreams, and I became fully aware of what they were doing.

Once I became accustomed to believing and acting upon my dreams, this ability led to another interesting development: my ancestors used my dreams to communicate with me.

Summary

Prophetic dreams became more prominent in my life as I was shamed into closing myself off to seeing spirits and scaring people. The dreams were personal—only I was aware of them—and I could pick and choose which dreams I wanted to share and with whom. While many prophetic dreams focus on disaster and danger, they can also be extremely helpful and instructional. Some dreams focus on the near future, while others foresee events in the distant future.

Exercise

Have you experienced any prophetic dreams? Describe the dreams in the space below.

_____

_____

_____

_____

_____

Should a person who receives a prophetic dream about someone else feel obligated to share the dream with the individual? Why or why not?

CHAPTER 5
NDE 2: FINDING HEAVEN

"There is only one path to Heaven. On Earth, we call it Love."

— Henry David Thoreau

In the last chapter, we examined prophetic dreams and how they appeared to historical figures as well as to my family members and me. Prophetic dreams became more prominent in my life as I began to mature. In this chapter, we will examine my second NDE, which occurred when I was twenty-five, twenty years after the first. This NDE shares many of the traditional traits described in other NDEs.

What led to my second NDE?

Have you ever been so sick that you thought you were going to die? Sometimes, it seems far easier to give up the ghost than fight for life. Often, surviving these moments come down to a single fragile thread that keeps us anchored to this realm. That is what I discovered in my second NDE. This soul journey took me to the brink of my earthly existence to see what was beyond the veil, and it gave me a choice between remaining on this plane or continuing my journey to the next plane.

Shortly after completing my training and probation with the Maui Police Department in 1978, I was assigned to the Molokai District as a patrol officer. We did not have a driver's licensing center on Molokai, so the job of giving road tests was assigned to on-duty police officers. Since I did not mind giving road tests to people, I began to take on that responsibility. This caught the attention of the director of licensing on Maui, who invited me to a week-long licensing seminar that was held at Northwestern University in Evanston, Illinois, in January 1979.

Having attended BYU Provo from 1972 to 1973, I thought I would be prepared for the cold Chicago winter. I was wrong. We arrived in Chicago just after a major blizzard hit the city. Over a two-day period, it left twenty-one inches of snow on the ground and was considered one of the worst blizzards in Chicago history.

I realized I would be in for a rough time when I stepped out of O'Hare International Airport from the baggage claim area to catch a taxi. I had borrowed a fleece-lined jacket with large plastic buttons for this trip. As soon as the buttons were exposed to the frigid Chicago air, every single one exploded like a firecracker! I was forced to stop at a store for safety pins so I could secure my coat. More concerns entered my mind when we arrived at our hotel. I learned we would have to walk a half mile just to reach the Northwestern campus. Had it been summer or spring, this would not have been a problem. Having to walk in inclement weather was not a wise choice for this time of the year. Lastly, the shoes I chose for this trip were too thin and the soles too slippery for the snow-covered sidewalks. I found myself slipping and falling several times on the way to and from the campus. The water from the melted snow seeped right through to my socks, making my feet wet and cold for most of the day.

By the second day of the seminar, I had caught a cold. As the week progressed, I developed chills and a fever. I found a better jacket and bought better shoes, but it was too late by then. I was already extremely sick. Despite this, I did not miss a day of the seminar.

After a cold, miserable stay in Chicago, I flew back to Hawaii. Arriving home to the humid air of Molokai compounded my illness. I was forced to take some time off from work to recuperate. A visit to the doctor confirmed my suspicions. I had double pneumonia.

I was placed on a heavy dosage of antibiotics and other medications to combat the infection in my lungs. Despite the medications, breathing was difficult, and my fever ran dangerously high. After three days of rest and medication, I showed no improvement. Finally, one evening, I was feeling so tired and drained that I told my wife, "I don't think I'm gonna make it. I feel like I'm gonna die."

I collapsed into bed and fell into an exhausted sleep.

NDE begins

I must have been asleep for a couple of hours when, suddenly, I felt something pulling at my toes. I tried to ignore it, but it kept happening. I opened my eyes and looked toward the foot of my bed. Standing there was my friend Bruce. Grinning from ear to ear, he was dressed in blue coveralls just as I remembered him.

"Wake up, sleepy head!"

Happy to see Bruce, I jumped out of bed and embraced him. We hugged each other and patted each other's back.

"Bruce, so nice to see you, man!"

"Nice to see you too, David John."

I finally realized how awkward this situation was. Bruce had been dead for just over a year.

"Whoa, Bruce, aren't you…?"

"Dead?" Bruce chuckled and smiled.

"Physically, yes, but no one really dies."

A feeling of dread overcame me.

"Does this mean I'm dead to?"

Bruce laughed as if he had heard a funny joke.

"David John, no worry; you're okay."

I then noticed Bruce had placed himself between me and the bed, effectively blocking my view of it. I moved slightly to the left and was shocked to see myself still sleeping in the bed.

"Oh, damn it! I am dead!"

I sank down to the floor and started to cry. Bruce started laughing again.

"David John, stop it. You're not dead."

"Then why am I here and my body is there?"

"Because I was sent here to show you something. I can take your spirit to this place, but not your physical body. Are you interested or what?"

"Where is this place?"

"It's inside there," replied Bruce, pointing to the bedroom closet. "You wanna see?"

Curiosity overcame my trepidation.

"Sure. Why not?"

Bruce smiled and chuckled as he walked to the closet. He slid the closet door open, then pushed aside my wife's clothes. This left an opening so I could see the closet's back wall. Where the wall was supposed to be gaped a dark hole, like the wall had been burned away. As I squinted deeply into the hole, I saw it was really a long narrow tunnel with a tiny speck of light at the end.

Bruce extended his hand to me and calmly asked, "You ready?"

I grabbed Bruce's hand. He led me to the tunnel entrance, and together, we stepped inside. Instantly, I felt a surge of energy coursing through my entire body. My breathing became easy. My headache disappeared, and I felt strong and vibrant again. I was amazed.

The tunnel was crooked and twisted, with many bends and corners. With every turn we made, the light in the tunnel grew brighter and brighter. The tunnel was unlike any earthly tunnel I have seen. The walls were more like a flexible membrane that gently undulated and pulsed like a living organism. The floor was soft and spongy like a wrestling mat. It felt as if I were walking through a giant blood vessel.

At one point in our journey, our garments changed. We both found ourselves dressed in white clothing that looked and felt like soft bird feathers. As I ran my hands over the material, it rippled in response, giving off an energy that made my body hum and vibrate.

Bruce and I discussed a lot of different things as we strolled through the tunnel, most of it dealing with my family and future. He was curious about my career choices, but he told me I would eventually figure things out for myself. He was not overly excited about my career as a police officer. He felt it went against my character.

We finally reached the end of the tunnel to which was attached a thin transparent membrane bulging outwardly like a bubble. This membrane separated us from what lay on the other side. The world beyond this membrane glowed bright and colorful, pulsating with an ethereal energy. The sky shimmered a magnificent shade of blue, the grass a vibrant green, and the soil a deep opulent brown. Fields of flowers ablaze with unearthly, radiant colors grew everywhere. Everything existed there so innately perfect and vivid. It was the most exquisite place I had ever seen.

Pets in heaven

As I marveled at the landscape filled with fruit-laden trees and showy blooms, I was surprised to see dogs, chickens, rabbits, pigeons, and guinea pigs dashing toward me. As they got to the membrane that separated us, I realized they were the pets I had raised as a child. There was Skippy, Spotty, Hector—my pet dogs—as well as Wheezy, my pet pigeon. I knelt and sobbed. How I missed my beautiful friends!

Family reunion

Suddenly, off to my right, a large group of people appeared. They approached the membrane and stopped about ten feet away. I immediately recognized family members who had recently died. In the group stood both sets of my grandparents, aunties and uncles, and a few relatives I knew only through photos. The crowd kept growing, and in no time, the entire landscape was filled with family members. Although I did not recognize all of them, I knew in my heart they were my ancestors. Most of them were smiling, and with hand gestures, they were inviting me to join them. I could feel their love and connection with me. This feeling of being enveloped in pure love and acceptance made me sob even more. I had never experienced a love so pure and profound, so forgiving, and unconditional. It brought me to my knees. It humbled me. It beckoned and welcomed me to stay.

Overcome with emotion, I felt a compelling urge to join my family and pets. I began stepping through the membrane. Immediately, Bruce grabbed me by the chest, stopping me in my tracks. Peering through the membrane, I saw my dad's father frowning, shaking his head, and mouthing, "No! It's not your time."

From the other end of the tunnel echoed the voice of my daughter Gigi.

"Daddy, where are you?"

With a heavy heart, I stepped away from the membrane, knowing I could not pass through to the other side. The image of my daughter stood out clearly in my mind. Despite knowing the beauty and love that awaits us all after this life, I knew I could not leave her. My little girl needed me. I had to go back.

My children Kawika (in walker) and Gigi at the time of my NDE in 1979.

"Where you think you going?" teased Bruce as he helped pry me away from the membrane.

"I have to take care of my family. I'm not ready for this yet."

Bruce gave me a big hug.

"Yeah, I know. I wish I had made the same choice you are making now."

I suddenly felt myself being pulled back through the tunnel. I popped up in my bed, wide awake, only to find my clothes and bed soaking wet. My fever had finally broken, and I was feeling much better. I got out of bed and warily approached the closet. Sliding open the closet door, I was shocked to find the clothes had been parted and I could see the closet wall. I quickly shut the closet door so the tunnel would not reappear.

How was my second NDE like other NDEs?

Many people who report NDEs talk about a person who guides them along a path that leads to a tunnel. The person who did that in this NDE was a family friend whom I admired, Bruce.

The second feature of this NDE was the appearance of a tunnel. The tunnel I experienced was not like a man-made tunnel made for cars. It reminded me more of slides found in water parks, with all the twists and turns in them. The tunnel's walls appeared to be part of a living creature.

The third feature of this NDE was the notion of a perfect world, with strong, healthy-looking plants, manicured lawns, perfectly blue skies, and warm weather. The colors were strong and attractive, almost like a painting created by a master artist. It seemed too perfect to be real.

The fourth feature of this NDE was the gathering of deceased family members, including pets. My grandparents and other family members who had died were on the other side, waiting to welcome me. I could feel their happiness and love. What surprised me the most was the presence of my beloved pets, who were my special friends while I was growing up. They were the most loyal friends I had ever had.

The fifth feature of this NDE was being overwhelmed by love. I had never felt so loved and welcomed in my whole life. I wanted to be part of that love and be embraced by it. It was exceedingly difficult to break away.

The final feature of this NDE was that I made the decision to return to life and was helped to return to this world by my love for my family. I did not want to abandon my children. I knew they needed me, and I needed them.

Summary

In this chapter, we examined the details of my second NDE, which most resembled other NDEs reported by other people. I was given a glance at what awaits me when I die, but I was also given the choice to live again. The key to keeping me anchored to the land of the living was my connection to my children and family.

Exercise

When you make your transition (after death), whom do you want to be your guide into the next realm? Why?

What family member(s) would you be most excited to see in this next dimension? Why?

_____
_____
_____
_____
_____
_____
_____

What pet(s) would you look forward to seeing again in this new life? Why?

_____
_____
_____
_____
_____
_____
_____

CHAPTER 6

TALKING WITH YOUR ANCESTORS

> "When we illuminate the road back to our ancestors, they have a way of reaching out, of manifesting themselves... sometimes even physically."
>
> — Raquel Cepeda, *Bird of Paradise: How I Became Latina*

In the last chapter, we looked at my second NDE and how it fits into the classical definition of an NDE. In this chapter, we will examine how your life could be impacted if you communicated with your ancestors on a regular basis.

How connected are you to your ancestors? Would you recognize them if they appeared to you in your dreams? Why is it important to connect with your ancestors? In this chapter, we will explore these questions.

Communicating with your ancestors is an ancient practice found in many cultures around the world, including Mayan, Celtic, Aborigine, Indigenous American, and Pacific cultures. Some major religions, such as the Catholic faith, honor the deceased on All Saints Day and All Souls Day with prayers, candles, incense, chanting, ceremony, and offerings. The desire to communicate with your ancestors is an innate part of the human experience. We intuitively sense their presence, which begs the question: Can we communicate with them?

Individuals can communicate with their ancestors through daily prayer, meditation, creation of art, music, food, and ceremony. Ancestors will respond through various forms, such as dreams, visions, or intermediaries, such as mediums. Your ancestor spirits can communicate, guide, protect, and heal the living. Your ability to connect with your ancestors is always available.

Some people confuse this desire to communicate with ancestors with ancestral worship; they believe that by communicating with your ancestors, you abandon God. This is not true. Communicating with ancestors and seeking their guidance is the same as speaking with them as if they were still living. Their deaths did not change our relationships with them. We love them and they love us. That does not change our relationship with God, our creator, whom we worship.

Finding my purpose

My second NDE introduced me to the realm of my ancestors. I was able to see who they were, all the way back to our beginnings. In subsequent dreams, I began to see more and more faces of my ancestors who had passed many years ago. I knew they were there, waiting for the right time to enter my life. Allowing that to happen was entirely up to me.

Why are your ancestors important?

One of my favorite lines from the film *Amistad* is spoken by Anthony Hopkins who plays the role of John Quincy Adams. In defending his client in court, he says:

"Who we are is who we were."

In searching for your own identity and purpose in life, you must consider who your ancestors were since all they ever were has been condensed into one person: you. You are the sum of all your ancestors before you back to the beginning of humanity. All their hopes, dreams, skills, and knowledge have been programmed into your DNA, waiting for you to awaken them.

Awakening your ancestors

A good starting point to awakening and inviting your ancestors into your life is learning about them through research and conversing with your family members. For me, rediscovering my family was part of my job as an educator. In 1990, I was hired as a social studies teacher at Kailua Intermediate School. My second year there, I started teaching Hawaiian Monarchy and Pacific Studies. As I prepared for my lessons and looked at the historical figures I would be talking about in my classes, I realized many of these people were my relatives.

I consulted with my brother Bill, who was also a Hawaiian scholar. He helped me identify many of our family members who played important roles in the establishment of our Hawaiian Kingdom. I went on a quest to learn as much as I could about my ancestors. I found them to be a group of talented healers, seers, leaders, and visionaries. As I learned more about them, I was determined to be like them.

Asking ancestors to teach you

Once you have gathered all the information you can about your ancestors, what do you do with that information? This would be a great time to ask them to participate in your life. How you want your ancestors to participate in your life is completely up to you. What are your goals and desires? How can your ancestors assist you in obtaining these goals and desires?

I wanted my ancestors to teach me to be just like them. I wanted to possess and learn all their skills and abilities that made them healers, seers, and leaders. To make that happen, I knew I had to ask them if they were willing to do that.

One day on my way home from work, I stopped off at the Pali Lookout and walked along the old Pali road. I entered the forest and found a secluded spot to pray. In my prayer, I asked my ancestors to teach me to be like them.

Have faith that your ancestors will respond

Later that evening in a dream, I was approached by a group of people dressed in various types of clothing from ancient Hawaiian times to the present. I knew they were my ancestors. Then a short, stout man with a full beard wearing a white *kihei* (cloak) stepped forward and addressed me. His attire revealed that he was a kahuna. This is what he said:

"There is no one person out there who can teach you what you want to learn. All our knowledge has been scattered, with bits and pieces found here and there. If you want to be like us, you must search for these bits and pieces and tie them together. We can help you with that."

"How do I know what to look for?" I asked.

"You will know when you see it."

"How do I start this?"

My kupuna reached down, picked up a round stone, and said, "Start here!"

He tossed me the stone and allowed me to study it. It was round and looked like a maika stone. A maika is a stone disk used in a game called *Ulu Maika*, which is like bowling. From a cultural perspective, I was starting with the basic building block of the universe, the *pohaku*, or stone, one of the early elements mentioned in the *Kumulipo* or Hawaiian creation chant. This dream established my connection with my ancestors. They agreed to teach me to be just like them.

Follow your ancestors' advice

I knew there were gathering protocols that needed to be followed if I wanted to work in shaping stones. I prayed and asked for guidance.

In a dream, I was shown what I needed to know. An old, white-bearded man took me to a secluded beach away from human encroachment. The more secluded the beach, the better, especially if I were going to use the stones for making bowls and poi pounders since they would be used to hold food. He told me if I were going to use the stones as maika, I could go to beaches near people's homes. Maika stones are not used to prepare food.

When we got to the beach, we introduced ourselves to the beach, and explained to it why we were there. We then asked permission of the beach, the spirits that guard the beach, and the stones themselves to gather only the stones we needed. For this trip, we were looking for stones we could shape into bowls and maika. I closed my eyes and saw the kinds of stones I needed to collect. After waiting a few minutes after our prayer, we began to comb the beach for the stones we needed. I was very particular about the stones since I already knew the sizes and shapes I needed. The only thing not clear to me was the type of stone. This is where picking up the stone, talking to it, and feeling its weight in my hand came into play. If it did not feel right, I let it go.

After collecting five stones, I called to my kupuna. He also had gathered some stones, but his were quite different from mine. His stones were flat and heavy. He told me that since I was shaping stones and wanted to keep things traditional, I needed shaping tools to form the bowls and maika. We both turned to the beach and thanked the spirits and the stones for cooperating with us.

As I walked away from the beach, I turned to my kupuna and asked him, "So, you gonna show me how to shape these?"

My kupuna laughed and said, "No. Somebody on Molokai will do that for us. Go home and find this man."

Finding the stone shaper

I flew home to Molokai and chatted with my dad. I knew his father, Grandpa Wallace, had been a stonecutter for the State of Hawaii. I remembered watching Grandpa shape poi pounders and wanted to know if my dad could teach me. My dad could not help me since he had not learned this skill from his father. Dad then directed me to the firehouse to talk with the old timers there. The firemen seem to know a lot about the people on Molokai since they have a lot of time on their hands.

I went to the fire department and spoke with the old timers to see if they knew anyone who still shaped stone on the island. They told me "Cowboy" Otsuka still shaped stone. I knew Cowboy because his son Lyle was one of my childhood friends.

I drove to Cowboy's home in Kamiloloa, Molokai. Fortunately, he was home. When I told him, I wanted to learn how to shape stone, his face lit up. He told me he had learned how to shape stone from one of my family members. Cowboy took me into his kitchen and opened his cabinets, revealing several poi pounders he and his children had made. They were beautiful. We then walked out of the house and went to a shaded spot near his garden where we sat in some chairs. He reached down to the ground and picked up a stone he was working on. He then grabbed a metal hammer head and began gently tapping the stone with it. With every tap, tiny particles of powder collected around the spot he was tapping. He stopped to show me how fine the powder was.

"This how you make 'em. If chunks of stone come flying off, you are hitting the stone too hard. You have to be kind and gentle with the stone, or the stone going crack."

Cowboy handed me the stone and hammer head and allowed me to shape the stone. After a few words of encouragement, I got the technique down. It was simple and easy but required a lot of patience. I spent a couple of hours with Cowboy, who patiently showed me the different techniques he used to shape poi pounders and bowls. He said to use the same methods to shape the maika.

Cowboy then shared an important concept with me: Choosing the right stone is the most important step in shaping it. For example, if I wanted to shape a maika, I needed to look for circular and flat stones that already looked like a maika. That way, most of the shaping has already been done by nature. The same rule applied to poi pounders. The proper stone for a poi pounder would be a cone-shaped stone that fit my hand.

Cowboy was incredibly happy that he could share his knowledge with me, a family member of the person who had taught him how to shape stone. It was like completing a circle. I now understood why my kupuna wanted me to learn from Cowboy.

Collecting my stones

After visiting with Cowboy, I returned to my parents' house and shared my experience with my dad. Before I went to bed, I prayed, asking God and my ancestors to help me find the stones I needed to shape my first poi pounder and maika. I also wanted to collect some stone-shaping tools.

That night, my bearded kupuna reappeared to me, this time showing me a baby eel.

"What is this?" I asked Kupuna.

Kupuna laughed. "Boy, go find your stones where this creature lives."

Before I could ask him anything else, Kupuna disappeared.

The next morning, while eating breakfast with my parents, I asked Dad if there was any place on Molokai associated with the eel. He looked at me and said, "Sure there is. Kepuhi Beach out by Kalua Koi."

"Thanks, Dad. I gotta head down there today."

Following breakfast, I borrowed my dad's truck and drove down to Kalua Koi. I parked as close as I could to Kepuhi Beach, which is directly in front of the hotel and golf course. Before getting out of the truck, I said a short prayer asking for guidance since this was the first time I would be collecting stones at this beach.

I walked down to the beach and introduced myself to the beach and the spirits there. There was a lot of sand, and not many rocks, but I was drawn off to my right toward Kawakiu Beach to the north.

Meeting my 'aumakua

As I started walking toward Kawakiu, I saw a large, thick, and long cloud form overhead. It looked like a long, thick rope. The cloud then shot quickly overhead, moving from Molokai toward Oahu. As I watched this happen, my eyes were drawn to the ocean. There I saw something exceptionally large and long skimming the water's surface. It was dark brown, spotted, and more than ten feet long and almost three feet in diameter. It was swimming in shallow water only ten yards from shore. At first, I thought it was a seal or dolphin, but it never popped its head out of the water, and I did not see any spraying from a breathing hole. I then realized I was looking at a giant eel!

The eel moved slowly along the shoreline toward Kawakiu Beach. I felt it was leading me somewhere, and my gut told me to trust this creature. I walked for almost twenty minutes, past the golf course, almost halfway to Kawakiu Beach. At that spot were lots of rocks.

The eel stopped, and then the sky went dark. I looked overhead and saw a large, long cloud blocking the sun. The cloud flew overhead from Oahu toward Molokai, then vanished. When I looked back to the water, the eel had disappeared, too.

Looking around and seeing all the beautiful stones I could choose from, I sat down on the beach and offered a prayer of thanks. As I prayed, I felt something jabbing my bottom. Ending the prayer, I backed away from where I had been sitting and noticed a small round stone that had a sharp point to it. I reached to pull the stone out but found it was only a tip of a larger stone, so I dug around it. To my amazement, this stone was shaped like a cone and fit my hand perfectly. It was as though someone had previously worked on this stone but been unable to finish it. Not too far from this stone, I found a very solid and dense stone I could use as a shaper. I also located four stones I could shape into maika. I found what I needed, so I offered a prayer of thanks to the beach and the beautiful eel who had helped me find the stones I needed.

When I returned to my dad's place and shared my experience with him, he reminded me his mother's family's 'aumakua was the eel (*puhi*) I had described. I later learned the name for our 'aumakua was Pukonanui. Pukonanui would appear as a large Moray eel or a long thick cloud, just as I had experienced at Kepuhi Beach. I felt very blessed that my family 'aumakua was willing to help me on my journey.

Shaping the stones

There is a three-day waiting period before you begin shaping the stones. During this time, if you have bad dreams about the stones, it means they changed their minds about becoming the objects you envisioned. You must return the stones to the place you found them. Following the three-day waiting period, since I had no nightmares, I began working on the poi pounder.

I wanted to honor my ancestors by shaping my stones using the traditional stone-on-stone method to shape my poi pounder. As I began to handle the stone, I felt an entity slip into my body. My eyes and hands began to move automatically, as if I had done this before. Suddenly, I was a spectator, watching someone else handle and shape the stone. This lasted for several days until I felt confident enough to work the stone myself. The entity then left me alone, and I was able to finish the stone by myself. It took me three weeks to finish shaping the poi pounder.

I then turned my attention to the smaller stones I had gathered to create maika. These stones were flat and circular, already resembling a disk, so I was able to finish shaping them into maika in two days. Every time I worked on the stones, I felt the same entity slip into me and help teach me what I needed to do. Once I felt confident, the entity left me alone to finish the job. The more I worked with the stones, the less the entity assisted me until, one day, I was left to do the work all by myself.

Communicating with your ancestors

Communicating with your ancestors requires faith, trust, and commitment. Your ancestors will test you and your resolve. Their goal is to bring out the best in you, which will often leave you dazed and confused. Many times, they will abandon you and allow you to fail if you need to be humbled. They want you to learn to solve your own problems.

The example of shaping stones I just shared with you represents one of the many ways my ancestors and I communicate with each other. When I need their help, I call on them to help me. If I need ancestors with specific skills, I make sure I mention the skills I need help with. I trust that the ancestors who step forward will be able to help me with what I need. If you are not specific about what you need, all your ancestors will show up, and that can be incredibly stressful and confusing for all involved.

It does not matter if you do not know your ancestors' names. They know you and are eager to help. When you find an ancestor you feel comfortable working with, ask them for their name so you can call upon them when you need them. These ancestors may appear to you in your dreams, visions, and meditations. They may also appear as signs in nature, appearing as clouds, a gentle breeze, a familiar odor, colors in the sky, or anything unusual that will capture your attention. You must be open and aware of these things that may occur right before your eyes.

When building this line of communication with your ancestors, you must show trust and follow through. You must develop faith in your ancestors and trust their impressions. You display this faith by following through and acting upon their guidance. Nothing is more frustrating than investing a lot of time and effort into helping someone, only to have that person ignore your suggestions. Why ask then? If you are having a difficult time hearing or communicating with your ancestors, perhaps a lack of trust or faith is the problem.

Feeding and respecting the ancestors

Once you establish a strong relationship with your ancestors, you can show them respect and reverence in several ways. How you choose to do this varies according to your culture.

Since having my experience with one of the *kinolau* (physical forms) of our family 'aumakua, the eel, I have decided not to eat eel in any form out of respect for our ancestor. My older brother Bill became terribly ill after eating eel on his trip to New Zealand, so it was a reminder to me that we are spiritually connected to this animal.

When I am having my meals, especially if my meals contain foods my ancestors savored like raw fish, poke, poi, taro, banana, roasted pig, chicken, *lau lau* (steamed pork and beef wrapped in ti leaves), and *'awa* (a bitter drink with a calming effect), I always make sure to pause before my meal and offer its spiritual essence to my ancestors. This act shows I am thinking about them and showing respect for their needs and desires. This creates a bond between me and them, strengthening our relationship. I am not worshiping my ancestors. I am caring for them as I would for any family member.

Here in Hawaii, some other cultures honor their dead by feeding them. I once attended a party at a Filipino friend's house. The family set aside a full plate of food on the family table that was reserved for their ancestors. My Chinese friends take full meals to the graves of their deceased relatives instead of taking flowers. I also see a lot of local families placing an open can of beer on their loved ones' graves. Offering food and drink to our ancestors is a respectful thing to do. Note to my descendants: When you come to visit me in the future, *Pake cake* (Chinese tea cookie) and a can of Pepsi are good enough for me!

Summary

In this chapter, we examined several ways you could establish your lines of communication with your ancestors. I shared my personal encounters with my ancestors and the various ways our ancestors can appear to us. We need to develop trust in our ancestors by following through on their promptings. Our ancestors include all human connections, as well as all elements in nature.

Exercise

Identify a deceased relative whom you greatly trust. What skills or areas of expertise did this person have? Do you think this person would reach out to help you in your time of need? Why or why not?

_____

_____

CHAPTER 7

NDE 3: MEETING DEATH

"That survival instinct, that will to live, that need to get back to life again, is more powerful than any consideration of taste, decency, politeness, manners, civility. Anything. It's such a powerful force."

— Danny Boyle

In the previous chapter, we examined how opening the channels of communication with your ancestors can lead to greater personal growth and acquiring hidden or lost information. In this chapter, we will examine my third NDE, the most unusual NDE of the four.

What would you do if you knew your internal organs were shutting down? What would you do if you knew you only had a few minutes to live? If death came calling during this time, would you have the strength and will to fight it off? This was my reality during my third NDE. This soul journey served as a wake-up call that jolted me into making needed changes in my life.

What circumstances led to my third NDE?

Teachers are very susceptible to illnesses their students bring into the classroom. Parents often send their children to school even when they are sick. Over the course of my career as a teacher, I have had more than my fair share of viruses and germs passed on to me by my students.

In 2005, I got dangerously ill again. I caught an illness from a couple of students who had vacationed in the Philippines and returned to Hawaii with a bug. After experiencing a fever and headaches, I decided to take a few days of sick leave to recover. It took only twenty-four hours at home to turn a simple bug into a life-threatening situation.

Although I was drinking a lot of water, I was unable to urinate. My temperature surpassed 102 degrees, making me dizzy and disoriented. When I tested my blood sugar, the level was so high my glucose monitor could not get a reading. I tried walking to my car with the intention of driving myself to the hospital, but I could not walk out of my apartment. The ambulance was called, and I was whisked away.

I was taken to Straub Hospital for examination and immediately placed in the ICU. The doctor who ran my tests looked overly concerned. He told me I had caught the avian flu. To complicate matters, I had developed meningitis and my diabetes had gone septic. I was awfully close to dying as my internal organs began to shut down. The doctor told me if I had arrived at the hospital any later, they could have done nothing to save my life.

My reaction to this news was odd. I really did not care if I lived or died. At that time, death would have been a welcomed relief. I had been battling depression for quite some time and had lost the will to live.

In the ICU, I was plugged into so many IV bags that the IV stand looked like a fully laden papaya tree. IV needles were in my arms, in my hands, and along my collarbone. I was so exhausted that I slipped into a deep sleep.

NDE begins

I found myself alone in a large graveyard, with rows of old headstones, leafless trees, and dried flowers on a handful of graves. It was the dead of night and pitch black, except for the light of the full moon and stars. Alarmed, I ran around blindly trying to find the exit, but instead, I managed to fall into a hole. Glancing up, I saw a headstone with my name written on it. I had fallen into my own grave! Fear gripped me in the chest, giving me enough strength to leap from the grave. I turned my fear loose on the headstone and tried to crush it with a couple of kicks, but I only managed to tilt it slightly to the left.

Suddenly, out of the shadows, a man appeared. He was tall and distinguished-looking, smartly dressed in a neat, black suit, white shirt, and dark tie. On his head sat a tall, black top hat.

"Hello, Mr. Wallace," said the man.

"Hello," I replied. "Who are you, and how do you know me?"

"I am called many things by different people, and I know everyone since everyone eventually gets to meet me."

"So, you must be...."

"Yes," he said, grinning. "I am Death, and I have come for you."

The hair on my arms and neck bristled as I looked Death in the eyes and yelled, "Fuck you! Leave me alone!"

Death rolled his eyes and sighed.

"Oh, dear. I thought you had been searching for me, so here I am. I have been watching closely the way you have been treating yourself. Your actions say you are ready for me."

Death stared into my eyes and stretched out his hand toward me.

"Come now, Mr. Wallace. It's time to go."

I panicked and sprinted away from Death. As I put a little distance between us, I paused to see if he was chasing me. To my horror, four huge, black canine creatures were charging my way. Red eyes blazing and teeth gnashing, they closed in on me. I turned and started to run, but I felt a sudden sting in the back of my right leg. Down into the ground face first, I went.

I kicked away from the first dog, then scrambled to a nearby tree where I felt I could defend myself. By the time I reached the tree, all four dogs were on me. I could feel them biting and tearing away at my flesh as I punched and kicked at them.

Suddenly, all my fear and anxiety evaporated. It was replaced by absolute and consuming rage. I felt my body transforming into something exceptionally large and powerful. I had changed myself into a giant werewolf! I towered over the dogs, armed with long sharp claws, powerful muscles, and a mouth full of bone-crushing teeth!

My appearance had no apparent effect on the dogs, who continued their attack on me. As the first attacker leaped high into the air to seize my throat, I snatched it out of the air and bit off its head. My eyes searched for Death and spied him watching in amusement close by. I spat the dog's head in his direction like a watermelon seed as I caught hold of another attacker. Skewering it with my razor-sharp claws, I shredded it to bloody bits like a Benihana chef. The third dog maintained a stranglehold on my right leg. I stomped on it with my left foot, turning it into a gruesome puddle of blood and fur. The last attack dog, witnessing what I had done to his mates, turned tail and ran away yelping.

I stood there facing Death, prepared to rip him apart if he decided to push me further.

"Come on, you fucker. Let's go now!"

Death took a couple of steps closer to me and began clapping his hands.

"Bravo, Mr. Wallace. Congratulations. I see you have found your will to live again."

"No act, you fucker! Let's finish it now!"

Death chuckled.

"There is nothing more to prove, Mr. Wallace. You made your point abundantly clear. You want to live, don't you?"

Sensing a softening of Death's grip on the situation, I relaxed and reverted to my human form.

"Yes, I do."

"Very well. As you wish," Death conceded.

With that, Death turned and walked away. After taking two steps away from me, he turned and looked back. Tipping his hat, he winked and said, "I'll catch you later."

Recovery

The end of this NDE was not the end of my ordeal. I spent another three days in the ICU fighting for my life. Finally, my vitals improved, and I was released from the hospital after seven days.

My struggle with death made me realize I had much to look forward to. I had finally met someone who accepted me for who I was, and I wanted to see where this relationship would lead me. I knew I needed to make more changes before I could finally accomplish what my ancestors wanted me to do.

NDE 3 Insights

This NDE was filled with many metaphors that illustrated the nature of my life at the time. The first metaphor was the old graveyard. It was unkempt and abandoned, dark and gloomy. Everything was dead and buried, no life to be seen. A fence surrounded it, giving me the sense of being trapped and unable to escape. That pretty much described my life at the time.

The next metaphor to appear in my dream was the hole I fell into, representing my grave. Fear blinded me, which led me to falling into the hole. Had I remained calm and rational, I could have avoided falling in. In real life, I was afraid and unsure of myself, doubting my feelings and promptings. This fear placed me in a pit where I was lost.

The next metaphor was Death itself. Meeting death allowed me to see him as someone who is impersonal and plays no favorites. Had I been ready to die, I think we would have enjoyed each other's company. It appears Death must abide by some rules, and for some reason, he allowed me to continue to live. This showed me that love and mercy rule our universe.

The next metaphor I met were Death's companions, the four large dogs. To me, they represented my fears of death that I needed to respond to. I could have turned timid and allowed these fears to overcome and devour me. That did not happen. I found the inner strength I needed to overcome my fears and defeat them. I needed to do the same thing in my real life—to find the strength needed to fight my fears and doubts and change my life for the better.

The final metaphor I was confronted with was the werewolf. During my childhood, the werewolf was the creature that frightened me the most. Interestingly, when I found myself in danger, I resorted to my greatest fear to save myself. Transforming into a werewolf required me to overcome my fear and realize I needed to become this feared creature to defeat the challenge I faced. Sometimes, when challenges are so great, we need superhuman strength and determination to succeed. This experience taught me that no matter how bleak things become, I can reach deep inside myself and adopt the persona I need to meet any challenge.

This NDE initially caught me by surprise since it reminded me that I am not a quitter. When I am cornered and out of options, my natural reaction is to come out fighting. I rarely run or back away from a challenge. My third NDE showed me that despite all the wrong happening in my life at the time, my life was still worth a fighting chance.

I clung to life with the hope that things would get better.

Whenever I am backed into a corner, I always find the courage to meet adversity head on. I can be kind and gentle, but if the situation warrants, I can instantly morph into a frightful foe. It is wise not to underestimate me if you push me into a corner.

Post-NDE

Following this NDE, I made several changes. First, I reestablished my connection with my ancestors, which I had put on hold for several years. I began to meditate and pray more often and called on my ancestors more regularly. I did more research into my genealogy, seeking to understand my ancestors on a more personal level.

Second, I began distancing myself from people who were interfering with my development as a spiritual being. These included some awfully close relationships with individuals I had known for many years. Walking away from these relationships took a lot of personal strength and determination, but I had to say "Enough. No more!"

Third, the most important change I made was finding someone to share my vision and values who supported me 100 percent. I found that person in my current wife, Elle. We were married on August 8, 2008.

I did not understand the significance of marrying Elle until we went to Molokai to get married. We wanted to get married on 8/8/8 because it is a very auspicious date for many cultures. I checked with several wedding performers here on Oahu, but they were all booked. I finally decided to check with a wedding performer on Molokai. She had an opening for the day and time I wanted to be married: 8/8/8 at 8:08 a.m.

Elle and I arrived at my dad's house on August 7. We were surprised to find my brother Bill and his wife Amanda at Dad's home. I had wanted my brother to conduct our wedding since he was a judge, but at that time, he was very weak and ill with cancer. I did not want to impose on him or his wife. When I told my dad that Elle and I were getting married the next day, my dad smiled and said, "Oh, how nice. You are marrying on my mama's birthday!"

It then dawned on me. My grandmother's name was Ellen, and my wife's name is Ellen. August 8 was not only our marriage date, but it is also Elle's birthday! Ellen Wallace meet Ellen Wallace. Nothing happens by chance. I now knew my grandma chose Elle to be my companion during this important time of my life. Grandma brought us home to Molokai to be with the family we loved..

Summary

In this chapter, we examined my third NDE, its meanings, and how it helped me make needed changes. I found new strength and determination to create something positive with my life. The most significant change this NDE brought was finding my wife Elle. By traveling home to Molokai to get married on August 8, 2008, I realized my grandmother Ellen played an important role in bringing me and Elle together.

Exercise

If Death approached you tonight, how would you respond?

_____

_____

_____

_____

What do you value in this life that would keep you from dying before your time?

CHAPTER 8
BECOMING A HEALER

> "Now, more than ever, our society is in need of sensitive and empathic people. Now, more than ever, the human race needs to go inwards and connect with the Soul again. As natural born healers, intuitives, and mentors, it is not only our responsibility but also our destiny to help humanity heal."
>
> — Aletheia Luna, *Awakened Empath: The Ultimate Guide to Emotional, Psychological and Spiritual Healing*

In the last chapter, we examined my third NDE and how it led me to my wife Elle. Meeting and marrying Elle served as a catalyst for change that transformed me into an entirely new person. It was the most important soul journey of my life. In this chapter, we will examine how I learned to become a healer.

Rediscovering the healer in me

Have you ever been given a simple task that served as an introduction to a greater challenge? It was a test, and receiving the next steps needed to complete the challenge was dependent on how well you completed the initial task.

I sensed that shaping stones was my ancestors' way of testing my commitment to becoming like them. As I developed my skills in shaping stones and coming into constant contact with my ancestors through the stones, I knew I had more to explore and discover. I did not see shaping stones as my primary work. I saw it as a lesson I needed to learn. That lesson was that stones are the same as people. To shape them properly, they must be treated with care and kindness. Mishandle them and they become broken. Once I discovered this lesson, I approached my ancestors in prayer, asking them for my next lesson in my quest to be like them. I received my answer a few nights later in a short dream.

In this dream, one of my ancestors approached me and said, "Imaikalani, look for these."

He held out his hands with palms facing me, then disappeared.

It was like a quick snapshot that appeared out of nowhere, but somehow it grabbed my attention. For several months, I struggled to understand the meaning of the open palms. At first, I thought the open palms represented people in church raising their hands in praise, so I visited several churches that did that. I could not connect with any of them.

Finally, one day while reading a community publication, *Penny Saver*, I saw a picture in an ad that showed two hands, palms facing outward. It was an ad for a free seminar on reiki held by a reiki master. I did some research about reiki and learned it focuses on using universal energy to heal yourself and others. I felt a strong desire to attend this seminar. Could this be the thing my ancestors were directing me to?

My first contact with reiki

The reiki seminar was conducted by Reiki Master Maureen O'Shaughnessy. About a dozen of us were there. We listened intently to Maureen give a brief description of reiki. Midway through the presentation, Maureen asked for a volunteer so she could demonstrate how reiki worked. I popped out of my seat and ran forward.

I had a selfish reason for this. I had a frozen right shoulder, something that had been plaguing me for several years. I could not raise my arm above my head. Maureen smiled and asked me to sit on a chair facing the audience. She placed both of her hands on my shoulders and continued to talk to the audience. I expected some sort of flashing lights or some strange surge of power through me, but there was nothing! After about three minutes, Maureen told me I was done and could take my seat. I was disappointed and returned to my seat. I lost interest for a few minutes.

After sulking a bit, I decided to rotate my shoulder. A loud popping and crackling sound occurred, like when you pop bubble wrap. It was so loud it alarmed me and several people sitting near me. When I rotated my shoulder again, the popping and crunching sound was a little less obvious. I could move my shoulder without any pain!

I stood up and walked outside to the hall. I decided to stretch my arm by walking my fingers up the wall. My arm stretched high up on the wall above my head. I then moved my arm around like I was warming up to pitch a baseball. I had full range of movement!

I started looking around to find something to throw and found a half-empty water bottle. I grabbed it, aimed it at a plastic rubbish can about twenty yards away, and threw the bottle. My throw had the snap and power I used to have before my injury. I ran back into the meeting room and asked Maureen, "Where do I sign up?"

I took the level 1 reiki class and discovered the world of energy healing. The more I studied reiki, the more I saw its connection to the Hawaiian perspective of a living, interconnected universe. I became a reiki master in 2005.

Reiki and the Hawaiian universe

As I studied reiki's advanced concepts, I understood why my ancestors wanted me to learn this healing modality. Many reiki principles match Hawaiian beliefs. For example, reiki teaches that the universe is animated with life. Everything is filled with energy, giving life to all things. Hawaiians believe the same thing. We are interconnected with all things in nature. Learning that Hawaiian values are part of a larger universal truth helped me embrace my cultural beliefs even more than before.

The healing teacher

By 2008, I had developed a reputation as "the healing teacher" among my students at Campbell High School. Since many of my students were athletes, they would come to my room with aches and pains after games, asking me to help them heal faster.

One of the most memorable healings occurred when the starting center for our football team, whom I will refer to as Jay, was injured during an OIA playoff game. He suffered a deep thigh bruise. His doctor would not clear him for the next game, which was to be played only six days after he received the injury.

Jay and a couple of his teammates came to my room during my lunch break seeking my help. Jay was on crutches and his thigh was heavily wrapped in ace bandages. He could barely move his leg. I asked Jay to remove the ace bandage so I could see the injured area. An oval-shaped, dark black bruise about the size of a small football was on the outside of his right thigh.

"You not using your thigh pads, eh?" I asked.

"No, they get in my way."

"So, Jay, what do you want from me?"

"I just want to see if you can help me."

I reminded Jay that I could not heal him. Only God could do that.

"Do you believe God can heal you?" I asked.

"Yes, Mister, I believe that."

"Very good. And when do you want to return to playing football?"

"Mister, the team needs me this weekend."

"Thank you, Jay. That is all I needed to know."

I then empowered my palms with healing *mana* (energy) while asking God for guidance in helping Jay achieve his goals. Jay covered his thigh with his shorts in preparation for the healing. I held both of my hands above the injury without touching Jay, and I allowed the healing energy to flow freely.

An immediate pull of energy from my palms went directly into the bruise. I activated my visualization skills to help break up the bruise. To do so, I imagined a large, stagnant pond filled with polluted water. This pond would represent the bruise in Jay's thigh. To this image, I introduced a flowing stream into the pond. As the fresh water flowed into the pond, I unclogged a blockage downstream so the stagnant water could be cleared out. I kept this imagery alive and moving in my imagination until I no longer felt the pull of energy from my hands. That took all of twenty minutes.

When the pulling of energy from my palms stopped, I asked Jay to roll up his shorts so I could examine the bruise. To everyone's amazement, the deep, dark bruise was gone, replaced by a light red mark that followed the outline of the former bruise! I asked Jay to stand, which he did without the aid of his crutches. He walked across the room and back without experiencing any pain. Jay hugged and thanked me, and so did his teammates. Jay was released by his doctor later that day, and he was able to play in the OIA playoff game that weekend.

Healing ancestors

As I began to develop my own healing insights and skills, I was reminded that I come from a long line of healers who have used their mana and faith to help others heal. Here are two stories about my healing ancestors.

My grandma, Ellen Wallace, was very skilled in healing, through using prayer, faith, and her knowledge of native herbs. During the Vietnam War, one of my cousins was drafted into the army. He was ready to be shipped out to boot camp when he broke a bone in his arm. It would prevent him from receiving the training he needed for the war. My cousin approached our grandma and asked her to help heal his hand. Grandma reset the bone and applied some Hawaiian herbs to the fracture. The bone healed in a couple of days, just in time for our cousin to enter boot camp.

My mother's family tells the story of one of our kupuna who lived in Kona. Like most people in Kona, our kupuna had a home near the beach, but also had farmland in the cooler uplands of Kona. To reach his farmlands, this kupuna would ride a horse along a well-marked trail. One night, after a big storm that washed away part of the trail heading to the farmland, he was riding on the trail when the horse stepped into a hole in the trail and broke its leg. Under normal circumstances, a horse with a broken leg would be shot and put out of its misery. Our kupuna did not have the resources to acquire another horse, so he decided to heal the horse instead. He dismounted and reset the bone in the horse's leg. He gathered some herbs he was familiar with, created a poultice, and wrapped it around the horse's fractured leg. He then prayed that the horse's leg would heal. He walked the horse to the farmland, where he worked for a few hours. When he had finished his work, he checked on the horse's condition. The horse's leg was healed. Our kupuna saddled the horse, then rode him home.

Tapping into people's energy

As a reiki practitioner, I depend on my clients to communicate with me regarding their needs. The pull or draw of the energy tells me where to focus my healing efforts, and what strategies I should use to deliver the needed healing energy. The more I work with a client, the clearer those perceptions become.

As I allowed my imagination to run its course, I soon found myself "seeing" inside the human body and describing what was happening to my clients' joints, muscles, and tendons. I could also see the major organs along with the colors and shapes associated with them. Sometimes, these "visions" would occur at the strangest times.

For example, once I was asked to perform a blessing on a home. After the blessing, my clients invited my wife and me to join them in a small dinner that included several members of her family. Elle and I sat at a table across from my client's in-laws. As soon as I sat down, I felt a powerful pull on my energy. My energy was being pulled toward my client's brother-in-law. I was feeling nauseated and uncomfortable, which made me genuinely concerned. To verify my suspicions, I closed my eyes and did a quick scan of this man. His lower left lung lit up like a tiny city at night. This was not normal.

Looking at this man, I asked, "Brah, you okay? How's your breathing?"

The man looked at me and said, "The doctors think I have pneumonia, so I am going back to check again next week."

"Pneumonia? Hmm," I replied. "Make sure you have your doctor check you out better, okay, or at least get a second opinion."

The man laughed at me, so I got the feeling he would just ignore me. Sensing that, I went to talk to his sister, my client, who knew about my abilities.

"Sista, you have to tell your brother that next week when he goes to the doctor, he needs to make sure his doctor takes his time and examines all the information he has about your brother. I think he is missing something."

"Really?"

"Yeah, your brother has something more serious than pneumonia."

"You think it's cancer?"

"I don't want to alarm anyone, but yeah, it feels like cancer, so it should not be taken lightly."

"Okay. Mahalo for letting us know. I figured it wasn't pneumonia."

A few days later, after the man visited his doctor, I got a call from his sister. The doctor changed his diagnosis to stage 3 cancer of the lungs.

Seeing my client's timeline

What would you do if, suddenly, you could see people's future just by touching them? Would you share your visions with others, or would you hide them out of fear? Would you risk the potential of being labeled a weirdo? This is the dilemma we all face when we attempt to share an incredible gift with the public. Not everyone will be ready for you.

As I continued to do healing sessions and investigate my clients' bodies, I began seeing flashes of my clients' futures. I would project my mind five to ten years into the future to see the kind of work they were doing. The biggest hint I received regarding their work was the clothing they wore. I saw many of my students in medical scrubs, military uniforms, or business suits.

One interesting case was when I worked with "Tony," a student of mine. He was an athlete caught between two sports: football and baseball. He was a wide receiver in football and an exceptionally good pitcher for our school's baseball team. When he hurt his shoulder, he asked me for help.

While I was giving Tony healing reiki energy, he spoke about being pulled between the two sports and asked my opinion on which he should focus on. After getting his permission to investigate his future, I received a quick vision of him: Tony was dressed in a Milwaukee Brewers uniform, pitching in a large stadium. This vision occurred during his junior year of high school and my last year teaching. Just over a year later, I received an article from Tony. He had been selected to play in a developmental baseball league in a team owned by the Milwaukee Brewers.

Tony was only one of many students I helped guide to the careers best suited for them. As my accuracy levels increased, I became greatly confident that I could develop my talents into something extremely helpful to other people.

Healing spaces and buildings

Have you ever walked into a place you have never been to and felt sick to your stomach? Did the place make you feel like running away and hiding? That is a clear indication something is not right with the building or place.

As I continued to expand my healing capabilities, people began contacting me to heal their homes. The homes I serviced were both new homes and homes that had served multiple generations or families. Each type of home presented its own challenges.

New homes

New homes built in areas where no other homes stood are often haunted by spirits who previously claimed the lands the homes were built on. The spirits can be transit spirits, walking along ancient paths, or resident spirits from previous times. In the Ewa Beach and Kapolei areas, many newer homes are being built in places once reserved for the dead in ancient times. New homes are encroaching on these lands. How would you feel if your neighbor decided to build their home over your house?

In these situations, my job is to find a compromise between the resident spirits and the homeowners. I ask the spirits to adjust their frequencies so that they do not scare the homeowners. I also educate the new homeowners about their behaviors so they can coexist with their spirit neighbors. A lot of problems develop in a home if a teenager is around since teenagers are more susceptible to spiritual influences.

Today's home builders do not consider the home's alignment with the environment and are unaware of the consequences of misalignments within the home. Doors, windows, mirrors, and hallways are all problem areas in the new homes I walk through. These misalignments lead to draining of resources, health issues, relationship issues, and energy problems. Some of these alignment problems can be fixed but require effort.

Older homes

Many of the problems I find with older homes have to do with the buildup of memories stored in a home's walls and floors. Whenever people meet and talk, fight, argue, or make love, these actions are recorded in the walls, ceilings, and floors of the rooms. These are "house memories." People sensitive to energy can pick up the energies tied to the house's memories when they enter these spaces. To remedy this situation, the new occupants need to do a cleansing and reprogramming of the environment. If this is not done, the old memories and energies can influence the new occupants. The same issues that plagued the previous owners may now become their issues.

Older homes also run into a problem when the previous owner dies in the home. Sometimes, the spirit chooses to stay in the home rather than leave.

For example, I was called to a home in Mililani that was sold to a young couple. The previous owner, a widow, had passed, and none of the family wanted to live in the home. As the young couple began living in the home, sometimes the wife would hear, late at night, the kitchen cabinet doors slamming, as if someone were angry. She and her husband would run down to check the kitchen, but no one would be there. After experiencing this for about a month, they called me for help.

When I entered the home, I could sense the presence of a frustrated, older Japanese woman. I did my checks of the living room, bedrooms, and bathrooms, and everything was okay. As soon as I stepped into the kitchen, I felt anxiety, like something was wrong. I looked around the kitchen and came to the sink. Dirty dishes were in it. I closed my eyes, and in a vision, I saw the old Japanese lady pointing at the dirty dishes!

I informed the young couple that the previous owner had kept her kitchen spotless. It had been her domain and still was. If they wanted the slamming to stop, they needed to keep the kitchen clean. Washing the dishes, putting them away, and keeping the countertops clean and uncluttered would establish peace in the kitchen. The couple did exactly what I asked them to do, and the slamming cupboards stopped. I have encountered this type of activity in many plantation-era homes I have visited.

People problems, not spirits

Most problems associated with haunted homes and places have little to do with spirits, with very few exceptions. Most of the problems are the results of people, their relationships, and the things they do or fail to do. They create their own problems by inviting unwanted or unneeded energies into their homes based on their own fears and ignorance. Guilt, envy, and jealousy can attract some extremely negative things into your home. I can measure these by listening to the way the people in the home address each other and how they react to me. I call these situations self-inflicted wounds.

Summary

In this chapter, we looked at my development as a healer and some of the skills I developed over time. My healing abilities began as a reiki practitioner and later developed to include reading a person's timeline and helping people clear their homes of spiritual or energy issues.

Exercise

A healer's first responsibility is to heal themselves. What physical or spiritual ailment do you presently suffer from?

_____

_____

_____

_____

_____

_____

_____

_____

To heal yourself, you will need to visualize yourself fully recovered from this ailment. Use the space below to describe your life once this ailment is healed.

CHAPTER 9

BECOMING A REMOTE VIEWER

"Intuition goes before you, showing you the way. Emotion follows behind, to let you know when you go astray. Listen to your inner voice. It is the calling of your spiritual GPS system seeking to keep you on track towards your true destiny."

— Anthon St. Maarten, *Divine Living: The Essential Guide to Your True Destiny*

In the previous chapter, we examined my development as a reiki healer, and how this healing ability expanded to reading people's timelines, seeing inside a person's body, and helping clear haunted homes. In this chapter, we will look at how I developed into a remote viewer by reviving a childhood ability.

What if you had the ability to project your awareness to any location around the world during any period, past, present, or future? What event would you want to observe? What would you do with the information you learned about the event? Are you aware that some people can do this on a regular basis? I am one of them. Our skill is called remote viewing.

What is remote viewing?

The International Remote Viewing Association (IRVA) defines remote viewing as a mental faculty that allows a perceiver (a "viewer") to describe or give details about a target that is inaccessible to normal senses due to distance, time, or shielding. For example, a viewer might be asked to describe a location on the other side of the world, which they have never visited; or a viewer might describe an event that happened long ago; or describe an object sealed in a container or locked in a room; or perhaps even describe a person or an activity, all without being told anything about the target—not even its name or designation. Remote viewing is related to so-called psi (also known as "psychic" or "parapsychological") phenomena such as clairvoyance or telepathy.

Remote viewing was developed in the United States by Dr. Hal Putnam, Dr. Russell Targ, and artist/psychic Ingo Swan in the 1970s. In 1978, the US government created a program that used remote viewing to gather information about our enemies around the world. It was extraordinarily successful. Following this success, multiple branches of the US military, as well as the CIA and surveillance communities, adopted remote viewing protocols to carry out their missions.

Becoming a remote viewer

Before I knew anything about remote viewing, I could see hidden objects if I put my mind to it. After being shamed for using this gift as a child, I purposely stopped using it unless it was needed. When called upon to use this ability, it was hit or miss, since I did not have a set protocol to access and use my gift. Eventually, I decided to mothball this part of my life until I could figure out how to make it more dependable.

Not long after becoming a reiki master, I had a strange dream. In it, I was taken to Pu'u O Mahuka Heiau, the largest ancient Hawaiian temple on Oahu, located in Pupukea. In the upper portion of the *heiau* (temple), stood a tall tower, made of bamboo, and wrapped with white cloth. A man dressed in a white kihei, revealing himself as a kahuna, invited me to the tower's front entrance. When I approached him, he invited me to enter the tower. Inside the tower, I noticed two Hawaiian men. One man was sleeping, and the other was talking to him. Although they were speaking Hawaiian, I understood what they were saying.

The sleeping man was describing a battle he was witnessing in his dream. The man who was awake was memorizing everything the sleeping man was relating to him. Occasionally, the awake man would ask the sleeping man to move to a different location and describe what he saw. I discovered that the sleeping man had somehow projected himself into the future and was reporting everything he saw to the man who was awake.

After a short time, the dream ended, and the sleeping man awoke. He sat up, looked at me, and said, "Remember what you saw."

He touched my third eye, and I woke from the dream. I had never seen or even heard about something like this before. I searched the internet for anything that could explain what I had witnessed, but I could find nothing remotely like it.

A few months later, I tuned in to the paranormal radio program *Coast to Coast AM*, hosted by Art Bell. Bell's guest called himself a remote viewer. This remote viewer began to describe a process he used while working with the US military to access Russian secrets. During the process, the viewer went into a meditative state and was guided by another person who was awake. The person who was awake was called a monitor. The monitor helped the viewer navigate his way around the intended target. This process was called a monitored remote viewing session, and it was exactly what I had seen in my dream. I knew that my ancestors had shown me the next step in gaining the skills I needed to become like them. I needed to become a remote viewer.

The Hawaiian equivalent to a remote viewer is a *kaula* (seer). This gift of extra sight and clairvoyance runs extraordinarily strongly in my family and is a common trait with me, my cousins, and my siblings. I see these gifts developing in my children and several of my grandchildren. This gift can display itself through dreams and visions.

A couple of days after listening to Art Bell's show, I went to a bookstore and found the book *Limitless Mind* by Russell Targ. In it, Targ suggests a simple process to test your viewing abilities. As I read Targ's book, memories of my childhood experiments with wrapped gifts and hidden objects flashed through my mind. I could do that as a child and young man, but could I do it as an older adult? To find out, I recruited my wife to help set up our first remote viewing experiment.

Awakening my childhood gift

My initial remote viewing experiment as an older adult was conducted on July 26, 2009, just over a month past my fifty-sixth birthday. Elle hid an object in a box while I was away at work. She did not tell me what the object was. When I arrived home, Elle informed me the target was ready, so I took out a notepad and grabbed a pen. I then focused on the box without touching it, and I allowed my mind's eye to see what was inside. A shape suddenly appeared in my mind, so I quickly drew a sketch that captured my first impressions of the object inside the box. This sketch is copied below. After completing the sketch, Elle and I opened the box and compared my sketch with the object in the box. The object was a white Crown Victoria conch shell.

The gift I discovered as a child had never left me. It was time for me to develop and expand it.

Sketch of hidden target, July 26, 2009

Target #1 Crown Victoria conch shell

This and other experiments aided by my wife eventually led me to being trained as a remote viewer by FarSight Institute (Dr. Courtney Brown), Coordinate Remote Viewing (Ed Dames), and the Hawaii Remote Viewers Guild (Glenn Wheaton).

To complete my training with the Hawaii Remote Viewers Guild in 2012, I was introduced to the monitored remote viewing session by my mentor Debra Duggan-Takagi. I lay on a mattress and drifted into a semi-trance state. Debra then gave me some verbal cues, which I followed. To this day, I am not sure if I was successful with my target because the suspect in the crime was never caught. Participating in my monitored session completed the assignment I was given by my ancestors.

Follow-up dream

A couple of nights after I completed the monitored session, I was again taken back to the tower at Pu'u O Mahuka Heiau in a dream. Once again, the Hawaiian man who had previously touched my third eye repeated the same words to me: "Remember what you saw." I said mahalo (thank you) to both men and left the tower with a feeling of satisfaction that I had not only understood what I had seen, but I had also experienced it firsthand.

As soon as I stepped out of the tower, I was greeted by a large host of Hawaiians dressed in their best traditional garments. I could see *ali'i* (chiefs) in their fine *ahu'ula* (feather cloaks), wearing colorful *mahiole* (feather helmets). I also saw *kahunas* (priests) in their white with dark trim *kihei* (cloaks). The entire upper portion of the *heiau* (temple) was a sea of feather cloaks and white kihei. The entire group said a short chant, raised their arms to the heavens, and shouted, "Eo!"

I stepped down from the tower mount and immediately knelt to pay my respects. A man dressed in a bright yellow feather cape, a chief, hurried forward and whispered to me, "Stand with your peers."

I looked up into this chief's eyes. Somehow, I recognized him. I rose to my feet, and we exchanged a *honi* (touching of noses), ending my dream.

As part of my soul's journey, I had successfully completed two assignments given to me by my ancestors. They realized I possess the tenacity to follow something to its completion, and the intelligence to interpret the clues they gave me. They accepted me as a peer among them, which earned me a spot to stand by their side.

Developing my remote viewing skills

As a member of the Hawaii Remote Viewing Guild, I participated in several interesting projects that proved I could describe targets anywhere, at any time. We worked on locating missing people, finding missing or lost items, tracking people and their movements, and locating hidden treasure. As I got better with these techniques, I found that working on some of these projects lacked real purpose, so I began to lose interest in them quickly. I needed something more meaningful. Then I was introduced to using remote viewing to play the lottery.

Why the lottery?

The odds of winning the Powerball or Mega Million lottery is just over 2 million to 1. The way I look at it, someone will win the lottery, so why can't that someone be me? Winning the jackpot for either lottery will help finance two of my dreams.

My first dream is building a home base for me and Elle. We want a place large enough to build our home, grow our gardens and fruit trees, and be able to produce much of our own food. We see ourselves in a rural, agricultural setting.

My second dream is to build a learning center where I can teach and practice my healing and energy work. This learning center will contain the needed structures and facilities to hold classes, workshops, retreats, and ceremonies. Hopefully, the land we eventually acquire will be large enough for both projects.

Challenges of playing the lottery using remote viewing

One of the major challenges I faced with remote viewing the lottery was the accepted belief among remote viewers, including my mentors in viewing the lottery, Dick Allgire and James Ferla, that numbers and letters are difficult to see. I accepted that belief to be true, so I looked for other ways to predict the lottery. Dick used a lottery ticket and would "see" where the winning numbers would appear on the ticket, while James used a directional method based on a technique we called S7 annex A. This technique uses our ability to sense the location of objects either in front of us, to our back, or to our sides to locate any object we may be searching for. James took this idea and applied it to identifying the winning numbers for the Powerball lottery.

I experimented with Dick's technique, but it did not work too well for me. James attempted to teach me his technique, but it was too confusing. Then one night, in a dream, I saw some familiar pictures I had learned back in the 1990s. These pictures were twenty memory pegs I had learned from a program called *Mega Memory*, sold by Kevin Trudeau. Each memory peg was associated with a number, 1 through 20. Here are the twenty original memory pegs created for *Mega Memory*:

Tree (1)   Pool (8)   Driver's License (15)

Shoe (2)   Baseball (9)   Candle (16)

Stool (3)   Bowling Ball (10)   Diploma (17)

Car (4)   Goal Post (11)   Vote (18)

Glove (5)   Eggs (12)   Golf (19)

Gun (6)   Black Cat (13)   Dollar Bill (20)

Dice (7)   Shovel (14)

If you examine each of these memory pegs, they make sense. For example, four tires on a car, five fingers in a glove, seven wins or loses in craps, and nine players and innings in baseball. There is a logic to the pairings of numbers and pictures.

Using the twenty memory pegs from *Mega Memory*, I could now use pictures to represent specific numbers. All I needed to do was program my mind to accept these picture associations with the numbers I wanted. That took time and practice.

Since I needed more than twenty numbers to play the lotteries, I spent several months organizing and testing different pictures and associating them with specific numbers before I finally got enough pictures to represent all the numbers played in the Powerball and Mega Million lotteries. Initially, the two lotteries had different number sets, but currently, they are almost the same lottery with the same number field to draw on. The final product I am using today is seventy pictograms representing the numbers 1 through 70 that I use to play any lottery I want.

Developing a protocol and format

Once I developed all my pictograms and was satisfied with them, I began to refine the protocols I used to predict each lottery. This was not a neat, linear process, but more of a series of trial and error, filled with confusion and self-doubt. I found myself in unchartered waters; none of my partners understood what I was trying to achieve, so they could not help me. Using the consistent set of pictograms for each lottery was not the way most remote viewers would do it. My mentors suggested using new pictures for every game I played. That seemed too cumbersome to me. I felt that numbers do not change, regardless of whether they are drawn in different lotteries, so why should my pictograms change?

Eventually, I discovered that since so many people were attempting to read the lottery's future drawings, it created a tremendous amount of noise that interfered with a clear signal. Somehow, I needed to separate what I was doing from the rest of the crowd. Here is where the idea of remote viewing my own drawings first crossed my mind.

Associative remote viewing

As I became frustrated with traditional remote viewing, I began to search for other forms of remote viewing that matched what I was trying to do with the lottery. This search led me to associative remote viewing (ARV). ARV is not considered remote viewing but a method for tasking your awareness to obtain information about the future. ARV uses photos that represent specific future outcomes to make predictions on binary events. Since I was using my pictograms to represent numbers, my method of working the lottery fell more in line with ARV.

An ARV session begins by the viewer focusing on *feedback*. Feedback is a time in the future when the correct sketch is created that represents the actual outcome of the event you are trying to predict. The challenge with ARV is how well you can communicate with yourself over time. Because you are focused on your own sketch that you will be creating on a specific piece of paper, you separate yourself from the noise created by everyone going after the lottery. This was exactly what I was looking for.

Below is a sample format I created to predict the lottery. The format continues to evolve, but the idea remains the same: focus on the feedback squares (bottom section) while drawing my preliminary sketch (top section).

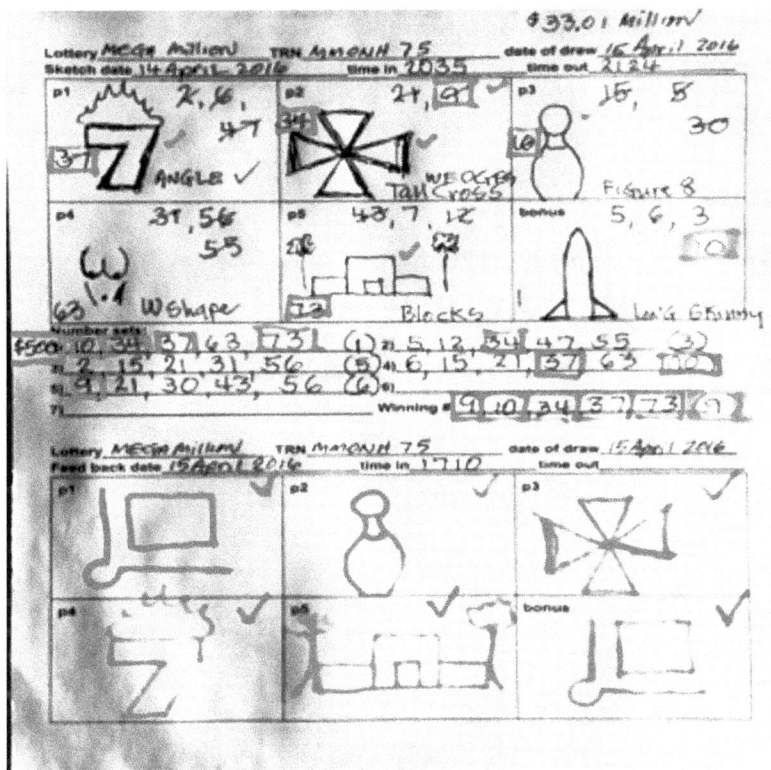

Mega Million Lottery worksheet, 15 April 2016. I correctly identified all six numbers drawn, placing four numbers on ticket A for a $500 win.

Using this format along with a specific set of protocols I follow for the Powerball and Mega Million lotteries, I have been very consistent in producing three or four numbers that are drawn on a specific date. I have identified all six numbers drawn several times, but not all the numbers were on the same ticket. I have produced some remarkable results with the California Fantasy 5 and Mega Million lotteries.

Summary

In this chapter, we examined my journey as a remote viewer and how it led me to my greatest challenge: winning the lottery jackpot. Developing my own method to predict the lottery has taught me patience and perseverance and tested my resolve. It has helped me develop the patience I need to work with my clients.

Exercise

If you had the ability to correctly predict the future outcome of any event, which events would you focus on?

_____
_____
_____
_____
_____

Would you use this ability to earn you some money? Why or why not?

_____
_____
_____
_____
_____

CHAPTER 10

NDE 4: FINDING YOUR PURPOSE IN LIFE

"The vision is true north for the soul. It is a permanent, intuitive compass direction for a human being. Every person inevitably strays from the path. Life is an endless experiment and course correction. The vision brings one back to the true path."

— Thomas G. Bandy

In the previous chapter, we examined my development as a remote viewer. Just as I began to grasp the concepts behind the art, I became extremely ill again. In this chapter, we will examine how this illness led to my fourth near-death experience.

Losing focus

Have you ever found yourself riding high on a wave of success, only to realize the wave you were riding was leading you to extremely dangerous waters? I found myself in that position as I began to expand my abilities into an area I was very fond of, shooting craps.

In 2007, I enrolled in a dice control training program called PARR and recruited Elle to be my partner in crime. I built a practice rig, consisting of a tossing and receiving station, and a ton of casino quality dice. I watched the videos and read everything I could about the game. I was obsessed.

While my precision tosses looked beautiful, I soon realized that to make money in craps would take more than tossing the dice with precision. You needed to know how to bet properly. Knowing how to bet and manage your bankroll is the key to being successful in craps. As I increased my table time at the casinos, I noticed I could sense when the seven was about to show.

As I began to develop my remote viewing skills, I looked for ways to use RV in my craps game. I began experimenting to see if I could accurately predict when the seven was about to show. To do this, I sat back and watched what normally happens when seven shows on a craps table. This is what I observed:

First, when a seven is rolled after a point is established, there is an emotional letdown. If there is a lot of money on the table, you may hear a few curse words. Every player who has a pass line bet, place bet, or prop bet loses, so not everyone is happy. Second, there is a massive chip movement away from the players toward the dealer. The dealer is collecting all the losing bets. The final clue that accompanies a losing seven is an empty craps table. All the chips have been cleared away, and the table is clean. Once I identified these indicators, I used my remote viewing skills to project my mind ahead in time to observe the players' emotions, chip movement, and table status following the next roll of the dice. If I sensed at least two of these indicators, I would call off my bets. The seven would appear within three rolls. It was very uncanny, and dealers at the tables noticed this right away.

As my skill in tossing the dice improved and my senses began to zero in on the game, I found myself being banned from several casinos for twenty-four hours. A twenty-four-hour ban is a tool that casinos can instantly enforce, without involving police, based on the discretion of any casino supervisor. This ban is used to sanction someone they think is breaking a casino rule. It can also be used to "cool" a hot player who is on a winning streak. During this time, the banned person can be prohibited from playing a certain game at the casino or could be banned from entering the casino property. For example, I could be banned from playing craps, but I would be allowed to play the slots. At first, being banned angered me, but I soon realized the casinos saw me as a potential threat. Being banned then became my badge of honor.

Since I was only a few years away from retirement for the Department of Education, I wanted to move to Las Vegas so I could take advantage of my skills at craps and other games I began to probe. The more games I played, I discovered that my ability to sense and read energy in people and places also applied to casinos. As I began making plans for my Las Vegas escape, my soul threw up a roadblock, giving me time to reconsider my purpose in life.

Sick again

In August 2010, I suffered three heart attacks while I was teaching at Campbell High School. Since I have type 1 diabetes, I did not have the classic signs of a heart attack, so I did not recognize what was happening. I felt tired, out of breath, and sweaty, so I thought I might be experiencing a sugar low. In the back of my mind, I suspected it was something more.

When I got home from work and told my wife what had happened, she convinced me to have a physical as soon as possible. It had been two years since I had last had one, so it was time. When I explained the symptoms of fatigue, feeling bloated, difficulty breathing, sweating, and overall malaise, my doctor made some on-site examinations and determined I was retaining a lot of water. He ordered a blood test and put me on Lasix to flush the extra fluids out of my body while we awaited the test results. He said he suspected I had congestive heart failure.

I lost fourteen pounds of water weight in a week taking the Lasix, and I felt so much better since my heart did not have to work as hard to push the extra fluid through my body. The blood tests, however, confirmed what my doctor had suspected. I was officially diagnosed with congestive heart failure. The tests also confirmed I had suffered a heart attack very recently. My doctor ordered me to go to the emergency room at Pali Momi in Aiea. I was immediately hospitalized and had an EKG done right away. The EKG confirmed I had experienced not one, but three recent heart attacks. An angioplasty was then scheduled; it revealed that three of the major arteries to my heart were blocked. I would need a triple bypass operation to correct it. The bypass surgery was scheduled for August 13, 2010. Pre-surgery tests revealed my mitral valve also needed to be replaced. That procedure was scheduled to be completed along with the bypass surgery.

As I mentally prepared for the surgery, I felt a sense of calm like everything would be okay. I did some research into the procedure and learned that the survival rate was quite high. I displayed all the classic symptoms associated with congestive heart failure: swollen ankles, shortness of breath, and difficulty walking longer than a few minutes. As I started to eliminate the extra water I was carrying, the swelling in my ankles disappeared, and I could walk for longer periods without resting.

The surgery

On the morning of August 13, 2010, I was wheeled from my hospital room to the surgical unit of Straub Hospital. I was told the surgery would take about four hours. Elle decided to wait for me until the surgery was completed.

I was amazed by the operating room's size, and soon realized why it was so large. Space was needed for all the people and equipment required to perform the surgery. As soon as the surgeon stepped into the room, I was put under anesthesia.

NDE begins

I remember a period of darkness, like I had fallen into a dreamless sleep. I do not know how long this lasted, but soon, I felt myself floating in the air and feeling very disoriented and confused. Just below me, I could see people with masks surrounding a person lying flat on his back on a small, narrow table. A lot of blue material was on the man, and I could see a large open gap in his chest, exposing his heart and lungs. I felt sorry for him.

Tension vibrated throughout the room as people quickly moved around the table. Wired paddles were placed on the man's rib cage, causing his entire body to jolt. I realized the medical staff was attempting to revive him.

As I moved closer to see if I could recognize the patient, I felt someone grab me from behind and yank me right out of the room. In an instant, I was outside the building, floating just above the hospital roof. I turned to see who had snatched me away and saw a Hawaiian man with a kind face. I recognized him from somewhere, but I was not immediately sure when I had seen him before.

My Hawaiian "captor" was accompanied by three tough-looking Hawaiian men I had never seen before. They sandwiched me between them as we zipped through space and entered a narrow winding tunnel. We soon arrived in an octagonal room I immediately recognized. Each side of the room had a door with a window. A bright light shined down on us. It was the same room I had been taken to as a child. The Hawaiian man I recognized was Kupuna from my first NDE.

The men had me sit on the floor. They then sat with their backs to me, effectively wedging me between them to limit my movement. I did not like the feeling of being trapped, so I began kicking at them to give me room. Kupuna looked at me and said, "Imaikalani, we are doing this for your own good."

"I know," I said. "But you guys gotta let me breathe!"

The men inched away slightly, leaving me just enough room to be clear of their warm bodies. I was still confused about why I was in this little room again, and why I would have four large men with me.

"Kupuna, why am I here and why are there four of you now?"

As soon as I uttered those words, a crowd of people gathered outside the room. Some of them came to the windows with drinks and food in their hands, showing them to me. I was hungry and thirsty, so I stood up and tried to walk past my guards. They stood up and closed ranks on me, once again leaving me no room to move. I pushed my hands between their bodies and tried to force my way through. No luck. I kicked at the back of their knees to see if I could hobble them. Again, no effect at all.

Meanwhile, the voices from the people beyond the room kept calling out my name, inviting me to join them so we could eat and drink together. I desperately tried to escape, even kicking my guardians in their groins. They stood their ground until I had completely worn myself out. I crumpled to the ground, defeated, and frustrated. They then relaxed and sat down on the floor facing me.

"Are you done now?" asked Kupuna.

"You fuckers, why can't I have a drink and something to eat? I'm hungry and thirsty, and those people are willing to feed me!"

"Boy, you forgot a lot of things, didn't you?"

"What do you mean *forgot*?" I grumbled.

"You forgot who those people outside really are."

I stared at Kupuna, who pointed to his eyes, and then closed them. Right! I needed to close my eyes to see who those people outside really were. I stood up and found a friendly face outside the room. I closed my eyes and with my spiritual eyes saw a hideous demon. Opening my eyes once more, I saw that all the faces outside the room were now the faces of demons. There were thousands of these demons who wanted to get their hands on my soul as if it were a trophy.

"Those are demons outside there. They want to take me away."

"Yes, that is correct. That is why we are here—to protect you."

Realizing what a horrible mistake I would have made if no one had stopped me, I hugged Kupuna, apologized, and thanked him.

"Does this mean I am out of my body again?" I asked.

"Yes, something is happening, so we felt it best that you rest here until things clear up, one way or another."

I did not like the way Kupuna said "one way or another." Something must be wrong. It then became clear to me that the man I had seen on the table being jolted by the medical staff was *me*. I quickly developed a huge knot in my stomach. Fear grabbed hold of me.

Sensing my growing anxiety, Kupuna began talking to me about my name again to distract me. Kupuna told me a new meaning to my name was unfolding. This new meaning placed me as one of God's peers so we could freely converse with each other and be co-creators and collaborators in the things we do here on earth. Because of that, much would be given to me and much expected in return. I realized I was being prepared for something especially important, a mission I needed to complete. He told me he approved of the way I was expanding my natural abilities without being afraid to use them to pursue my interests. He warned me that by stretching and applying myself to nontraditional areas, especially gaming, I would draw the ire of many people who thought I was misusing my gifts. Kupuna assured me my gifts were mine to use and develop in whatever ways I saw appropriate. I did not need anyone else's permission or approval. Kupuna reminded me that our ancestors loved gambling and used it to test their mana (energy). He encouraged me to work on my inner vision since it was another key to understanding what Imaikalani means.

Kupuna's voice was hypnotic, so I found myself nodding off to sleep as I momentarily entered a dark silent chamber. Seconds later, I felt myself falling. I briefly woke to find myself in a small room with tubes running down my nose and throat. IV bags hung to both sides of me. Nurses stood nearby, talking to me, even though I could only respond by nodding yes or no.

I dozed in and out of sleep, unaware of the time or where I was. I knew I was in the hospital, but everything was hazy. I knew I had survived the surgery and was no longer in danger.

Lessons learned from NDE 4

In Mormon belief, when we die, our spirits go to a place referred to as paradise where we wait to be judged. Everyone, from the most innocent to hard core criminals, are placed there. From my first and fourth NDEs, I discovered multiple places a spirit can journey to, depending on who is guiding them. In both incidents, I became afraid of the circumstances I faced and needed a safe place to calm myself down. My ancestors responded by taking me to a safe room where they watched me.

Despite being in a safe room, I learned that the spirit world is filled with tricksters and detractors who will purposely lead you astray. Although these entities may have friendly faces, their real intentions can be very dark. You really need to be careful whom you trust and associate with in the spirit realm. My first and fourth NDEs taught me a legion of demons wants to stop me from accomplishing my mission in this lifetime. I am blessed with an active crew of protectors who constantly shield me from these harmful entities.

A loving light, which I call the light of God, shields and protect us if we choose to stay in the light. The walls and doors of the room I found myself in allowed me to make my own choice. I could have left the room by simply opening the door. My companions, who were experienced in this realm, persuaded me not to.

Finally, the sacred meaning of my name was emphasized again. I was reminded that I have a sacred duty to perform. It was important for me to stay focused and complete the task I was given. The weakening of my physical body forced me to strengthen my spiritual body and mind.

Road to recovery

My scheduled four-hour surgery took seven-and-a-half hours to complete. When I asked the surgeon why it took so long, he simply responded, "There were complications."

One complication was that an artery the surgeon wanted to use for my bypass was clogged and could not be used. Veins were taken from my leg to complete the bypass. Another complication was something no one spoke to me about. After gaining consciousness, I noticed my chest and abdomen was covered with round bruises. It looked like I had gone twelve rounds with Joe Frazier. I was beat up badly. These circular bruises were from the paddles to restart my heart. The medical team had gone through an epic ordeal to restore my life. It made perfect sense that my kupuna would shield me from seeing this.

After recovering in the hospital, I was released to spend more time to heal at home. During this time, I understood why Elle was brought into my life. I was as helpless as a child and depended on her for all my needs. It was the first time I trusted a woman to care for my every need. The bond I developed with Elle during this time helped define us as a couple.

During this healing period, I took a serious look at myself and asked, "Who am I, and what do I want to be remembered as?" The answer: I wanted to be remembered as a teacher, healer, and seer, not as a gambler. I put my heart and soul into developing my healing and remote viewing skills, which helped me heal faster. While I still enjoyed craps, it was no longer an obsession. I started to balance my activities between the spiritual and material worlds. By the time I returned to work, after three months, I was a different person.

Summary

In this chapter, we looked at how my fourth NDE served as a course correction for me because I had strayed from my main purpose in life. I gained better insight into the spirit realm and established a deep bond with my wife.

NDE 4: FINDING YOUR PURPOSE IN LIFE

Exercise

What is your life purpose? Do you have any deep desire to accomplish something? What is it, and why is it important to you?

_____

_____

_____

_____

_____

_____

_____

What skills or gifts could help you achieve your life purpose? How will you acquire these skills or gifts?

_____

_____

_____

_____

_____

_____

_____

_____

CHAPTER 11
BECOMING A KAHU

"Ku'ia kahele aka na'au ha'aha'a."
(A humble person walks carefully so as not to hurt others.)

— Native Hawaiian saying.

In the previous chapter, we examined my fourth near-death experience and some of the lessons I learned from this experience. In this chapter, we will discuss the transformation I experienced when I decided to accept my ancestors' invitation to become initiated as a *kahu* (a steward or caretaker).

Gifts from your ancestors

What would you do if your ancestors approached you bearing gifts that would change your life forever? Would you jump at the opportunity, or would you be cautious and take time to consider these gifts? If you accepted these gifts, what would you do with them? Who would teach you how to use them? I faced this situation as the journey of my soul intensified.

In early 2014, I met Roy Goya, a medium from Maui. In Hawaii, many of us call our elders our uncle or aunty. It is a sign of respect between generations. Since Roy Goya is my elder, I call him Uncle Roy. In our conversation, Uncle Roy informed me that two entities were standing by my side who had some important things to share with me. The first was a woman holding a wooden bowl with a yellow kihei tucked inside the bowl. She stood to my right and was offering both items to me. The second person, standing to my left, was a very prominent and distinguished man who had been important during his lifetime. This man wanted me to "step into his shoes" and become "initiated."

As Uncle Roy described the woman, I immediately recognized her as my grandma Ellen. She was offering me the symbols associated with our family's spiritual connections. Accepting those symbols would mean I agreed to carry on our family's spiritual traditions.

After a moment of reflection, I understood that the distinguished man Uncle Roy described had been appearing in my dreams and visions since I was a child. His name is Hewahewa. He lived from 1774 to 1837 and was the *Kahuna nui* (spiritual advisor) of Kamehameha I and II. Stepping into the shoes of a Kahuna nui would not be easy. I would need to master ten skills to do this. I could already do eight of them. The other two skills were ceremonial and could be learned.

Following my conversation with Uncle Roy, I reached out to my grandma and Hewahewa through prayer and accepted the gifts and challenges they were placing before me. I asked for their help in manifesting these gifts in this present world. Since I did not understand what being initiated meant, I asked my ancestors to introduce me to a person who would know what it meant. The answer to my prayer came in the form of Kahu Kaiwi, another medium from Waimanalo, Oahu.

After I explained my situation to Kahu Kaiwi, he invited me to be initiated as a kahu. I did not fully understand how becoming a kahu would help me achieve what my grandmother and Hewahewa wanted from me, but it felt like the right thing for me to do. It was a step in the right direction.

During the 2014 March equinox, I was scheduled to be initiated as a kahu near Kaena Point, Oahu. I was asked to perform an *'awa* ceremony to open the initiation process, something I knew nothing about. 'Awa is a drink made from the dried roots of the piper methysticum plant. The dried roots are either chewed or pounded into powder, then mixed with fresh water in a large wooden bowl. This mixture is then served in a special cup to guests. 'Awa ceremonies are often held in conjunction with other events such as weddings and birthdays, honoring visiting guests, and starting a business venture. They can be very ritualized. The ceremony is often used to unite people before any major event.

Creating my apu 'awa, or 'awa cup

I prayed to my ancestors to show me what I needed to do to prepare for the ceremony. In a dream that night, I was shown a coconut shell cup that was cut open lengthwise, rather than being split along the center of the shell. I woke up the next morning wondering where I could get a fresh coconut. Not many coconut trees grew in Wahiawa where I lived. I closed my eyes and asked to be shown where I could get a coconut. I was directed to the produce aisle of our local Foodland store!

Elle and I went to Foodland and bought several coconuts that had already been husked. I came home and began cutting the coconuts in the same fashion I was shown in my dream. We made enough *apu 'awa* (ceremonial 'awa cups) for me and a couple of the other kahu who would be initiated.

Initiation dream

Upon finishing the apu 'awa, I had another dream. In it, I saw myself standing near the shoreline of a secluded beach. I was wearing a yellow kihei and had a long bushy green lei draped around my neck. The ends of the lei touched the tops of my feet.

I found myself facing the ocean and chanting, while holding a bowl filled with 'awa. As I gazed into the ocean, I could see two large upright boulders, one to my left and one to my right. When I finished the chant, I immediately walked to the boulder to my left and poured a cup of 'awa on the boulder. I turned toward the mountains where I saw two other upright boulders to my left and my right. The four boulders marked a boundary for a sacred space. I approached the back two boulders and shared 'awa with them. I walked back toward the shoreline and fed the boulder to the front right. Completing the ceremony, I then offered 'awa to the kahu conducting our initiation, followed by offering it to the other kahu according to their ages.

In the dream, I was shown how to dress for the ceremony, where I should stand when addressing the sacred place, and how I was to share the 'awa. I had already gotten my yellow kihei, but I did not know where I would find a lei that could come close to the lei I saw in my dream. While the lei looked like maile, a traditional leafy vine plant used for lei in Hawaii, it had the feeling of a ti leaf lei.

Receiving my ti leaf lei

I was still teaching at Campbell High. It was the Friday before our spring break. My initiation as a kahu was scheduled for the following Saturday. I had called several lei stands to see if I could get one of them to make a lei just like the lei I had seen in my dream. No one had gotten back with me, so I was resigned to wearing a kukui nut lei to the initiation.

Since it was a catchup day at school when no instructions were given to the students, I decided to allow my class to watch movies or play games if they did not get too rowdy. While sitting at my desk, I had the sudden urge to go to our copy room. I stood up, told my students I would be stepping out for a few minutes, and made a beeline for the copy room.

As I walked into the room, I noticed our Hawaiian language *kumu* (teacher) was using the copy machine. Seeing each other, we exchanged a *honi* (touching of noses, a formal greeting) and started a conversation. He asked me about my plans for the upcoming break, so I told him I was being initiated as a kahu a week from Saturday. He was incredibly happy and congratulated me as he finished his copying. I left the room and went back to my classroom. I sat down on my chair and asked myself, *Now what was that all about?* I discovered the reason forty-five minutes later.

There was a knock at my classroom door. One of my students opened the door and a young lady holding a plastic bag stepped into the classroom. When she asked for Mr. Wallace, I waved my hand at her, and she walked back toward my desk. She then handed me the plastic bag and said, "This is from Kumu."

I took the bag, thanked the student, and told her to extend my mahalo to Kumu.

I untied the bag and looked inside. In it was a beautiful ti leaf lei woven to resemble a maile lei. I stood up and took the lei out of the bag. Draped around my neck, the ends of the lei touched the tops of my feet. This was the lei I had dreamed about.

I sat down and cried like a baby, overwhelmed with emotion. My students saw me bawling, so they all came to my desk looking concerned. I told them why I was crying and stood up to show them the beautiful lei Kumu had created for me. They were touched, but not as much as I was. The arrival of the lei was confirmation I was doing exactly what I was supposed to do.

When I visited Kumu in his classroom to thank him for the lei, he told me he had been compelled to make a lei, but he had not known who it was for. He had even brought extra ti leaves to school to make the lei longer because he felt the person who was to receive the lei was taller than he was. When he ran into me in the copy room and found out I was to be initiated as a kahu, he understood who he was to give the lei to.

Initiation day

On the day of the initiation, Elle and I drove to Kaena Point from the Mokuleia (north) side. When all the initiates arrived, we went to the beach to cleanse our bodies. After cleansing, we returned to our cars and dressed in our ceremonial kihei, along with leis and *haku* (head wear), if we had them. I took out my lei, which looked and felt magnificent.

We walked along the trail to Kaena Point. As I walked, a familiar figure appeared to my left. It was my brother Bill, who had passed on in 2009. He was dressed in a yellow kihei, remarkably like mine, and wore a haku lei on his head. In his right hand, he carried a tall wooden staff. He wore a mischievous grin on his face that I did not know how to interpret, but that he had come to support me warmed my heart.

Wrong place

We finally reached our destination. After laying down our mats and implements, Kahu Kaiwi asked me to begin the initiation with the ʻawa ceremony. Standing at the spot Kahu Kaiwi selected, I mixed the 'awa and turned toward the ocean. Everything looked wrong. I could see the boulder to my left, but I could not see the boulder that was supposed to be on my right. I turned to Kahu Kaiwi and said, "We're in the wrong spot. We need to move."

I walked closer to the shoreline and around a small hill until I saw the landmarks I had seen in my dream. I turned to Kahu Kaiwi and said, "This is the right place."

We moved our mats and implements to the new location before I started the 'awa ceremony. I completed the ceremony exactly as my ancestors had instructed me. The initiation process proceeded smoothly, and we left Kaena Point feeling very blessed.

Planning for retirement

The earliest I could retire was June 2015. As I investigated the future to find out what I would be doing, in visions and dreams, I saw myself speaking before groups of people. The groups would vary in size from two to four people to rooms filled to the brim. As an educator, I am accustomed to speaking to crowds of people, but I did not fully understand why people would be interested in listening to me. In every vision, I saw the people listening to me were mostly women, with a few men here and there.

Voice in the car

One day, while driving home from Ewa Beach to Wahiawa along the H-2 freeway, a voice spoke to me from the backseat of my car. It was a familiar-sounding male voice.

"Imaikalani," the voice said, "go to your kumu's house and humble yourself before her."

I had taken chanting classes from a female teacher who lived up the street from me, so she was the only kumu I had recently worked with.

"You want me to go to Ai'ai's house and humble myself to her? Why?"

My right ear stung with pain, as if someone had just flicked it with their finger.

"Just do it, boy; no ask why!"

"Okay already!"

I drove into Wahiawa, past my home, and went to my kumu's home. As I pulled up in front of her house, she was sitting in her carport as if waiting for me. I walked up to her, knelt before her, and explained that a voice had told me to humble myself before her. I lowered my head and told her, "I am your *kauwa* (slave)."

We both embraced and shared our love and respect for each other. Later that evening, I had a short dream in which my kupuna were pleased that I had done what they had asked. I was told my attitude toward women needed to change, and this act showed my willingness to make the change. Not until a few years later, when I began teaching Ha Ki'i, did I realize more than 99 percent of my students and clients would be women.

All the events and circumstances that occurred with this initiation process validated my efforts to honor the gifts and challenges given to me by my Grandma Ellen and Hewahewa. Becoming a kahu allows me to access, use, and expand the spiritual powers of my lineage. The primary role of the Kahuna nui is to use their mana to advise and counsel people. My role as a kahu allows me to do exactly that.

My mission as a kahu

A kahu's main role is to be a servant and caretaker. I have spent a large portion of my adult life as an educator, teaching and helping to guide my students to become positive contributors to our society. It is something I do very well.

As a kahu, I have accepted the responsibility of educating and training people to use and expand their natural abilities in diversified ways. Reiki and Ha Ki'i Medical Intuition and Healing are available for those who want to cultivate their healing abilities. For those who want to learn how to see hidden things or find missing objects, I have a simplified method of remote viewing. For those who want to beat casinos at their own games, let me teach you how to read slot machines, see cards before they are dealt, and pick numbers that will be turning up on a roulette wheel. If you want to play the lottery, I have three different methods you can use to win.

Beyond teaching and training, I serve as an advisor, life coach, and advocate for people experiencing problematic areas in their lives. These challenges can be physical, mental, emotional, or spiritual. My services in these areas include psychic readings, healings, cleansings, and blessings for individuals, homes, or businesses.

Summary

In this chapter, we examined my journey to become a kahu. This journey was made possible by the guidance I received from my ancestors and key individuals placed in my path at the right moment in time. Everything aligned correctly to help me fulfill this important transition in my life.

Exercise

Identify a personal goal your ancestors can assist you with.

_____

_____

_____

_____

_____

_____

_____

Once you accomplish this personal goal, how will you use your newfound skills or abilities to help others?

_____

_____

_____

_____

_____

_____

_____

_____

CHAPTER 12
HA KI'I HEALING

> "The loving personality seeks not to control, but to nurture, not to dominate, but to empower."
>
> — Gary Zukav

In the last chapter, we discussed my journey to become a kahu. In this chapter, I will share the core beliefs and teachings of Ha Ki'i Healing as channeled to me in dreams and visions by my ancestors and guides. This chapter contains part of my manual I use in my Ha Ki'i Healing workshop.

Are you interested in developing your ability to heal yourself and others? Do you want to learn how to tap into a pure source of energy that will empower your healing abilities? Have you considered the role our ancestors play in our healing ourselves and others? If any of these questions spark your interest, then this is a must-read chapter for you. If you are already an experienced energy worker, you may want to place a bookmark here for easy reference.

Ha Ki'i revelations and visions

By 2012, I had completed training as a remote viewer and had become an established reiki master. I had completed every assignment my ancestors had asked of me. I was ready for the next task. In a series of dreams and visions, my ancestors challenged me to create a new way of helping people heal. I was to accomplish this by combining reiki and remote viewing skills. They gave me the name Ha Ki'i for this new practice and left me to figure out how to make it work. Their guidance was offered whenever I hit a snag or lost my way.

The name Ha Ki'i is comprised of two Hawaiian words: ha and ki'i. Ha is the life force in all human beings. Ki'i means image or picture. Based on the meaning behind these words, I realized this new practice would involve reading the ha energy in a person. Using my ability to see hidden things, I would then receive a mental image to help me locate and describe the sources of illness or pain in the human body.

As a practicing reiki master, I could already feel and read the ha energy in my clients and understood what this ha energy was trying to communicate with me. The ha of a person told me if they were well or ill and pointed out the areas that needed my attention. Besides interpreting the ha energy in people, I also possessed the ability to see inside a person's body. This ability often allowed me to locate and spot injuries my clients suffered from. This skill alone, however, was inconsistent.

Applying remote viewing to healing was a natural transition for me. Remote viewing gave me the discipline and structure I needed to read consistently and accurately what was happening within a human body.

Between 2012 and 2014, I worked to merge everything I knew about reiki with Hawaiian practices and remote viewing to form the foundations of Ha Ki'i. The results were a method of medical intuition and healing that were divided into three parts.

The first part of Ha Ki'i is Ha Ki'i Healing. This form of energy healing has its roots in reiki but includes unique concepts such as cooperative healing, while using a pure source of healing energy.

The second part, called Ha Ki'i Medical Intuition 1, focuses on helping people understand what is happening with their illness or injury by conducting an in-person health scan that looks inside the human body.

The final part, Ha Ki'i Medical Intuition 2, uses the same application as Ha Ki'i 1, but it is done from a distance using a proxy. This allows a practitioner to perform a health scan on a person anywhere in the world.

Ha Ki'i can be a stand-alone practice, or it can be used in conjunction with other energy practices. In 2015, I conducted my first major Ha Ki'i workshop in Nauvoo, Illinois. The workshop was sponsored by the Grandmothers Healing Circle.

The following excerpts are from my Ha Ki'i Healing Manual.

HA KI'I HEALING

A HEALER'S ROLE

Healers are people who possess the knowledge, desire, talents, and personality to help others who are ill. Their lives have been one of service to others, caring for others. The desire to do the same has led many of you to this point in your life where you are reading these words. Some healers focus on people, others focus on animals, and yet others focus on the environment. Whichever you are attracted to, the healer's role is the same: to make things right so harmony and happiness can be achieved. How healers do that will depend on their knowledge, skills, training, and experience. This class will provide you with a specific perspective on what it means to be a healer and how to enhance your abilities as one.

BUILDING BLOCKS TO BECOMING A BETTER HEALER

Three principles exist to becoming a better healer: intention, attention, and expectation. Let's briefly look at each one.

Intention: Your intention must be clearly and precisely stated. Your intention gives life and energy to everything you do as a healer. How do you want the universe's healing energy to be used? Where and on whom do you intend to use this energy?

Attention: When you are working on a client, you need to focus your attention on the client and be aware of every reaction or lack of action your client experiences. You will also need to pay attention to the environment and what is happening around your client. If you are using herbs or any other healing aid, you will need to be sensitive to how it may impact your client and the healing process. You will also need to pay attention to your own limitations, understanding what you can and cannot do. Attention to the smallest detail will help tremendously in the healing process.

Expectation: Your expectations should be linked to your intentions. Expectations are the end results you want to see when you first visualize what you want to accomplish. Expectations go beyond mere visualization. When you expect something to happen, you are certain it will. This becomes an exercise in faith.

CODE OF CONDUCT

1. As healers, we hold our clients' names and conditions confidential. Information shared among healers regarding our clients during training sessions must be approved by our clients.

2. Always gain permission from those you are about to heal. Exceptions are parents who approach you to heal their child or incapac-

itated patients. If a patient is incapacitated, get permission from the person responsible for the patient, i.e., a spouse or parent.

3. Know your limitations. Do not promise things you cannot deliver.

4. Do not let money, or the lack of money, deter your healing responsibilities. It is okay to accept donations, *ho'okupu* (gifts or offerings), or charge a fee if you are depending on this work for your livelihood. Be sure your fees are reasonable. It is reasonable for families to pay travel-related fees if you are called to areas beyond where you live.

5. You are encouraged to incorporate your own cultural/religious ideals into your practice along with what you are learning through Ha Ki'i. Make this healing process yours.

ACCEPTING THE HEALER ROLE

I know many of you are reluctant to labeling yourselves as healers, seers, psychics, etc. I shy away from this myself, though I will use these terms on my flyers or business cards. While this humility may seem like the right attitude to have, we forget that we are servants, not masters. The skills, training, and talents we choose to develop are not for us alone, but to help others. To better help others, we need to feel comfortable being recognized as healers.

WE HEALING

The most important philosophy embraced by Ha Ki'i Healing is *We Healing*. We Healing is a healing technique based on partnerships and cooperation. It is a collective effort that is initiated by a healer, who then summons their healing partners to help in the healing process. The partnerships we will explore today are: Energy, God, Angels, Ancestors, Self, Clients, Environment, and Family. Once the partners are summoned, the healer channels their intent through the partners. Each partner then adds their own gifts and abilities to the healing process, multiplying the healing powers of the collective.

Energy

When we examine the basic building block of everything in the Universe, we arrive at one item: energy. Energy is the oldest force in the universe; it existed before the concept of God or the Creator. This energy is neutral and filled with potential. To release this potential in energy requires intent. Since energy can be shaped and formed by our intent, it becomes our first partner in healing.

To master the art of healing, you need to understand energy's nature. Energy flows to where it is needed. Where there is a void and need, energy is drawn. Those who are ill or injured require more energy to heal so they will pull and draw energy toward them. Healthy people do not need extra energy, so they will not draw energy toward themselves. Sometimes, healthy individuals will exchange energy with you, and you will feel a "push" from them, or energy moving away from them toward you. You can use this directional flow of energy—the push or pull—to get a general impression about a person's health.

Po, the source of pure energy

For Polynesians, the source of all life in the Universe emerged from a place we call Po. Po is a place of dark matter that created the building blocks for everything in our Universe. The creation of our Universe did not use all the materials available in Po. There is much more than we can even comprehend.

While the physical location of Po has been debated, I believe Po exists in all living things in our Universe. Po is outside of us as well as inside. Traveling to our personal part of Po to access healing energy involves an inward journey to discover our own power and light, which is already there.

Connecting to the environment's energy

Take the time to become aware of the energy around you and available in nature. Feel the power of the wind, the warmth of the sun, and the joy of a leaf laughing on a tree. Breathe in the air and feel the life force that enters your body with every breath you take. These are your partners in healing. Reach outward and become aware of everything around you. Walk slowly and observe. Take your time and read what is happening around you.

As you become aware of the energies around you, you will find yourself attracted to certain places where the environment seems to respond to you best. For example, I am always drawn to Keaiwa Heiau in Aiea since I am remarkably familiar with the energies there. If you decide to create your own space, in your home or on your property, dedicated to healing, this area will attract the type of energy you will need. When you develop a relationship with these energies, you will have a cooperative partner to help you.

God Creator

Raw energy is neutral, shapeless, and formless, but contains tremendous potential. God Creator is an energy force with intelligence. It is a higher form of energy in the universe. To be useful, raw energy needs to be formed and shaped by intelligence that has intent. Energy existed before God, but when God emerged, this intelligent creator shaped energy into the universe we now occupy. Since God created all things in the Universe and we continue to be shaped and molded by this energy, we need God's cooperation to be successful healers. We assist God in God's work by helping our fellow creations overcome ailments that keep them from fulfilling their part of God's plan on earth. God Creator Spirit is another partner in healing. We connect to God Creator through prayer, chants, or meditation. We all have our own way of doing this through our cultural or religious background.

Angels/Spirit Guides

Another important partner associated with We Healing is angels or spirit guides. These spiritual helpers from a higher plane of existence provide us with guidance and assistance when we need them.

The Archangel Raphael is the angel of healing. Prayers and protocols are used to call upon him for his assistance. In the Catholic tradition, there are many patron saints of healing who focus on a specific illness or condition. For example, St. Dymphna is the patron saint of depression and mental illness, while St. Peregrine is the patron saint of cancer. For addictions, there is St. Maximilian Kolbe while St. Jude is the patron saint for lost causes.

Spirit guides or guardian angels are personal spiritual attendants who have been with us from the time we were born. Some of us are aware of them, but others may not be. Some are permanent attendants while others will drop in occasionally, depending on our needs.

Spirit guides or guardian angels have one job: to guide and inspire us if we allow them to be part of our lives. Messages we receive from these beings are often referred to as the "still small voice in us." Sometimes, these messages will appear in our dreams or meditations. As we learn to listen to these promptings, the messages will come more frequently and with more detail. The more we develop trust with our guides and guardians, the more they will participate in our lives.

Connecting with angels, guardian angels, or spirit guides is a personal experience. You can make this connection through prayer, meditation, or simply asking for their permission.

Ancestors

Polynesians and other Native peoples will relate to the concept of ancestors better than the concept of angels or guardian angels. When speaking of ancestors, I am referring to three different groups of ancestors. The first group is viewed in the same light as patron saints or family guardians often referred to as ʻaumakua by Hawaiians. This group of ancestors is our protectors. The second refers to direct ancestors who live inside you and contributed to your DNA. They are inside of you and are always present in your life. They have great interest in your life, since you represent all they ever were. These ancestors are more likely to respond to you when you call on them. The third is a group of ancestors who are related to you but not in your direct line, like uncles and aunts. This group of ancestors come and go according to your needs.

Many ways exist to connect to this group of helpers, including through prayer, meditation, and your dreams. Hawaiians have several chants that were composed for that purpose. The chant I use is "Na ʻAumakua" which was adapted from David Malo's book *Hawaiian Antiquities* and modified to meet our needs today. This chant is a *mele pale*, which asks for protection and spiritual clearance before you begin a difficult task.[1]

---

1 https://apps.ksbe.edu/olelo/sites/apps.ksbe.edu.olelo/files/Makahiki%204%20Mele%20Pale-N%c3%a4%20%e2%80%98Aum%c3%a4kua.pdf

Na ‘Aumakua

Nā ‘aumākua mai ka lā hiki a ka lā kau

    Guardians from the rising to the setting of the sun

Mai ka ho'oku'i a ka hālāwai

    From the zenith to the horizon

Nā ‘aumākua iā kahina kua, iā kahina alo

    Guardians at my back, in front of me

Iā ka'a ‘ākau i ka lani

    At the right side of the heavens

O kīhā i ka lani, ‘owē i ka lani

    A whisper in the heavens, a rustling in the sky

Nūnulu i ka lani, kāholo i ka lani

    A reverberating above, rapidly moving in the sky

Eia ka pulapula a ‘oukou ‘o _____.

    Here is/are the descendants of you, _____.

E mālama ‘oukou iā mākou (māua, ia'u).

    Take care of us (3+) (us 2, me)

E ulu i ka lani, e ulu i ka honua

    The heavens shall grow, the earth shall grow

E ulu i ka pae'āina ‘o Hawai'i

    The Hawaiian Islands shall grow

E hō mai ka ‘ike

    Give us knowledge

E hō mai ka ikaika

    Give us strength

E hō mai ke akamai

> Give us intelligence
>
> *E hō mai ka maopopo pono*
>
> > Give us the right understanding
>
> *E hō mai ka ʻike pāpālua*
>
> > Give us the second sight/intuition
>
> *E hō mai ka mana.*
>
> > Give us spiritual power.

Self

To be an effective healer, you must be prepared to perform your role to the best of your ability. You must be prepared mentally, physically, and spiritually. Know your limitations, what you excel in, and what areas you need to improve. Do not make promises you cannot keep.

Clients

As healers, we need to make sure we are in tune with our client's needs, mentally, physically, and spiritually. Spend time listening to your client and asking questions regarding the illness or injury so the healing energy will be directed and used in a way appropriate for the client.

All clients who agree to participate in the We Healing process will be given a set of instructions to follow. They will be required to do some pre-healing cleansing and preparation, as well as a set of procedures during and after the healing session itself. These directions are found later in this chapter.

Be aware that not everyone wants to be healed. Some clients have established their identities based on their illnesses, so being healed will eliminate the attention and care they have become dependent upon. Being ill benefits them so they have no desire to get well.

Environment

Healing occurs best in an environment conducive to healing and wellness. Be sure to thoroughly examine the room or home of a person recovering from an illness. Remove any distractions that may interfere with the healing process.

Family

Family plays an important role in helping a person recover from an illness. Everyone in the family needs to agree to allow their family member to recover as quickly as possible from their illness. Be sure family members are contributing their love and healing thoughts to their loved ones who are ill.

We Healing is all encompassing and requires the cooperation of many levels of consciousness and awareness. The more in tune we become with the interconnectivity of all living things, the more effective we will be as healers.

WE HEALING PATIENT PROTOCOLS

A copy of the below guidelines is to be given to your client before the healing session takes place.

Dear Client:

Healing is a cooperative effort between a healer, client, God, angels, ancestors, your environment, and the Universe. As a person who will be receiving this healing effort, here are a few things you are asked to do before receiving your healing session. We also have a set of protocols for you to complete once you leave the treatment center.

Before Healing Session:

1. Give yourself permission to be healed.
2. If you were injured by someone else, forgive that person and release all hostile or negative feelings toward them.
3. Free yourself from any blame or belief of karmic debt you think you owe.
4. Purify yourself if you feel it is needed. A simple way is to cleanse while you are showering. As the water flows over your body, imagine all the negative energies attached to you being washed away from your body and going down the drain.

At the Appointed Time of Healing:

1. Before the healing session begins, connect yourself to the Universe's energies. See yourself among the stars, connected to all living things in the Universe. Allow the energy of the Universe into your life. As it begins to flow into your body, direct this energy to heal the specific areas that are injured or ill.
2. Invite God to help you by being part of the healing process. Extend this invitation to your guardian angels, saints, or family members.
3. Grant permission to the healer you are working with to conduct this healing session.

4. Believe and expect healing to occur.

5. Meditate for twenty minutes, reciting the sound "om" with each breath you exhale. Om is the same sound in *home*, without the H sound. This sound works better when it is said "internally."

End of Session

Say a prayer of thanks to your team of healers. Your healer will call you for a feedback session within two days of the healing session.

Mahalo nui loa. Thank you for allowing us to serve you.

Healer Preparation

It is highly recommended that healers cleanse themselves before conducting a healing session. Ritual cleansing allows us to begin focusing on the task at hand and clearing away mental or spiritual blocks we may have. There is no one right or wrong way to cleanse. Use a method that suits your needs and beliefs.

Determining a Place for Healing

As you perform more healing sessions, you will develop a preference for where the healing session is to occur. If I were to perform a live healing session, my first place of choice would be Keaiwa Heiau. If my client is extremely ill and cannot make it to Keaiwa, I would be obligated to travel to where he or she is located. If the person lives on a different island, or on the Mainland, my healing method of choice would be distance healing using a photo or proxy. Over time, you will realize many advantages exist to distance healing. In Ha Ki'i Healing, no difference exists between in-person and distance healing. Both are conducted the same way.

DAY OF HEALING

Connecting to the Universe:

As part of the preparation process for the healing, both healer and client visualize themselves connected to the center of the Universe, drawing in energy from this cluster of stars. Expand your awareness outward and feel the oneness that exists in nature.

Connecting to God:

Healer and client ask God to participate in the healing process.

Connecting to Angels, Guides/Ancestors:

Healer and client ask their angels, guides, and ancestors to participate in the healing process.

HEALING SESSION BEGINS

Light a candle

The lighting of the candle will be a signal to your conscious mind that the healing session is about to start. The candle and its flame will be used later to purify any negative energies we extract from our client. The erect candle and flame represent *ku*, the male energy of healing. If you want the female energy of healing to be present, you will need to have a bowl of fresh water. This will represent *hina*, the female energy of healing. The flame and the water are good cleansing elements you can use during your healing session.

Prepping hands for healing energy

We start the healing session by first cleansing our left palm using our right thumb by drawing the Cho ku rei reiki symbol (see Chapter 13). After cleansing the left palm, we move to our right palm and repeat the process.

Connecting to Po

Take the time to reconnect to Po. Allow the pure energy of Po to concentrate in your heart. Once in the heart, we give purpose to this pure energy. We turn it to healing energy with our intentions. Converting our Po energy to healing energy, we direct it down both of our arms and release this energy to our client.

With every breath we inhale, we draw in pure energy from Po. With every breath we exhale, we release healing energy through the palms of our hands. This is the natural rhythm, the ebb and flow, of healing energy that we are channeling.

Healing team visualization

Take time to visualize your healing team. See the universe above you, God to your right, angel(s) to your left, and your ancestor(s) across from you, creating your own healing circle. In the middle of this circle is your client. Your team of healers will be mirroring everything you do from this point on.

Opening/clearing of healing channels to client

Extend your right hand toward your client. See all your team members doing the same. Form a cup with your right hand and begin clearing away any energy blocks your client may have to their aura. This clearing is done by imagining your hands and the hands of your team members are scrapers or scrub brushes that are removing any blemish in your client's energy field. As you scrub your client's front, your ancestor will be cleaning your client's back, God will be cleaning the left, and the angel will be cleaning the right. Move from the top of your client's head and down to the bottom of their feet.

As you clear away these blocks or negative energies, cast them into the flame of the candle or bowl of water you prepared earlier.

Application of healing energy

After clearing your client's aura, you are now ready to apply healing energy. The application of healing energy follows a natural rhythm.

With every breath you inhale, you will be drawing raw energy from Po and the universe into your body. As you inhale, allow the raw energy to enter your heart. Once it reaches your heart, tell yourself, "Convert this energy to love and healing." As you exhale, allow love and healing to be released from your heart, down both of your arms, and outward to your client through the palms of your hands. Do this three times, repeating "Convert this energy to love and healing."

Breathe at a natural pace. Do not rush, and do not hold your breath. Relax.

To increase the flow of energy to your client, rock your hands slightly to the right and left. Movement increases the intensity of the energy leaving your hands.

Remember, everything you do is being mirrored and repeated by your team of healers.

Duration of healing session

A healing session will consist of three five-minute focused healing segments with a short two-minute break between segments. This will take up about twenty minutes of your time.

Feedback and completing the healing cycle

Your first healing session with a person will probably be live and in-person. Following this session, spend some time with your client to see how the client responded to the session. Based on your feedback, you can set up a schedule for the final segment of the healing cycle, which consists of three complete healing sessions. The severity of the illness or injury will decide how many healing cycles the client may need.

Following the initial live session, the remaining sessions will take place through distance protocols. You will go through the entire process you used in the live session, only this time, you will imagine your client is sitting in the middle of your healing circle when you decide to initiate the distance healing.

I recommend you do the distance healing sessions when your clients are all sleeping. The advantage of doing distance healing is you can have *all* your clients included in your healing circle if you want to.

Summary

In this chapter, I shared with you the manual I created for my Ha Ki'i Healing workshop. It contains the main philosophies, beliefs, and protocols established for Ha Ki'i Healing. For more details about this workshop, please contact me via my website at www.IntuitiveInsightsHawaii.com.

Exercise

What personal qualities would you look for when trying to select a personal healer for you or your family?

_____

_____

_____

_____

_____

_____

CHAPTER 13
HA KI'I MEDICAL INTUITION

"You will never follow your own inner voice until
you clear up the doubts in your mind."

— Roy T. Bennett

In the previous chapter, I shared with you a manual I created for my Ha Ki'i Healing workshops. This manual identified the philosophies, beliefs, and protocols of the Ha Ki'i Healing method I organized. In this chapter, I will be sharing some of the processes and protocols I use as part of my Ha Ki'i Medical Intuition practice.

What would you do if you had the ability to sense a disease or illness in a person? Would you share that information with them? What if they got angry at you and called you a weirdo? Would that hurt your feelings? What if your reading were wrong? Would you give up and walk away from trying to develop this skill? These are just some of the issues you must learn to deal with while developing your skills as a medical intuitive.

What is medical intuition?

Medical intuition is a system of expanded perception built upon human intuition. Using this expanded perception, a practitioner is able to intuitively assess imbalances in the body's physical and energy systems.

These systems include the aura, chakras, and biofield. Medical intuition can be used in assessing the influence of thoughts, beliefs, and emotions on an individual's health and wellbeing. Medical intuition is not to be mistaken for the practice of medicine, psychotherapy, or any other licensed healthcare practice. It is not a replacement for medical care, diagnoses, therapy, counseling, or any kind of treatment.[1]

What role do medical intuitives play in healthcare?

A medical intuitive's primary role is to help calm the fears of people afraid to see a medical doctor. The intuitive can inform the person of their findings and assist them in receiving the proper care they need. Many professional medical intuitives are already working with doctors in the United States.

One of the first cases I worked on as a medical intuitive was a mother and daughter I met in Waikiki. The daughter had developed some lumps in her right breast, and since the family had a history of breast cancer, the mother was convinced her daughter had cancer. The fear of cancer gripped this young lady, but she refused to see a doctor. However, she did not mind seeing me, a psychic intuitive.

After getting this young woman's permission, I focused my attention on her right breast. I did not have to touch her but relied on my vision and imagination to do my work. Just below her skin, between the skin and layer of fat and muscle, I saw an unusual cluster of yellowish spongy tissue. It did not have any blood vessels feeding it, so it looked more like some extra fatty tissue. It did not look or feel like cancer.

"Excuse me, miss," I said calmly. "This does not look like cancer to me. It looks more like some extra fatty buildup in your breast."

Both mother and daughter burst into tears, overcome with relief.

---
1 https://www.thepracticalpath.com/what-is-medical-intuition

"To be sure, please make an appointment with your doctor to get a breast examination, okay?"

"I will, kahu. Thank you so much."

Two weeks later, I received a call from the daughter. She had gotten a breast examination and was checked by her doctor. The lumps in her breast were indeed fatty tissue and no threat to her. My impressions were correct, and this woman received the medical care and confirmation she needed.

What is Ha Ki'i medical intuition? Where did it come from?

The Hawaiian art of the Kahuna Ha Ha served as an inspiration for me to investigate the field of medical intuition as my reiki awareness expanded. The Kahuna Ha Ha were experts at diagnosing illness in the human body using their sense of touch. Of all the Hawaiian healing modalities, this art form most captured my imagination.

I was already receiving images and impressions from my reiki clients as soon as I touched them. As I attempted to mimic the works of the Kahuna Ha Ha, my ancestors directed me in a dream to use the two skills I had already developed: reiki and remote viewing. Merging these two disciplines helped me focus on my strength—my ability to see hidden things.

As I developed a rudimentary form of the Ha Ha practice, my ancestors approached me in a dream and gave me a name for this new practice: Ha Ki'i. The term Ha Ki'i describes a process I use in healing and detecting illness or injury in the human body. Ha is the life force present in every human being. Ki'i means image. In working with my clients, I can read their ha energy, which is then viewed as a "vision" in my mind. This vision, accompanied by a flow of energy to the affected area, helps me locate and describe pain or illness in my client's body.

Key components of Ha Ki'i medical intuition

Belief

To function properly in any role, we need to believe we can perform the tasks we are called upon to perform. You need to believe you can read energy and see hidden things and that your readings are accurate. Trusting the methods and protocols designed for this method and repetitive practice reinforces your belief in your abilities. If you have problems believing, you probably need to practice and exercise your skills more. To sharpen your skills, I have designed several exercises that practitioners are encouraged to use every day.

Using your hands

Our hands are the most important tools in Ha Ki'i. We will be using them to read the ha energy and to send healing energy when needed. You will be at an advantage if you have been reiki attuned to level 2 since you will already be trained to send and receive energy through your hands. Attunement is not needed for Ha Ki'i Healing.

Procedures:

1. *Clearing and cleaning your hands:* Before you begin your work using your hands, you must clear the hands of any negative energies and blockages. To do this, wash your hands thoroughly with a mixture of spring water and sea salt. While washing your hands, ask God and your ancestors to help prepare your hands for the work you are about to do.

2. *Energizing your hands:* To empower your hands, use the Cho ku rei symbol from reiki and draw the symbol three times on both palms of your hands. I use my thumb to draw the symbol. The meaning of Cho ku rei is "place the power of the Universe here." Cho ku rei is the catalyst that gives power to all the other reiki symbols.

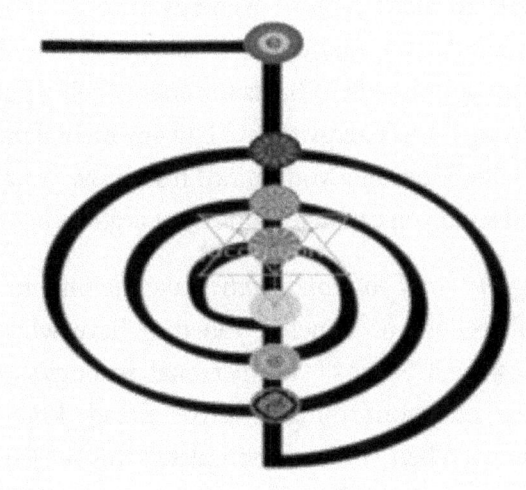

Reiki symbol Cho ku Rei

3. *Channeling energy through your hands:* Focus your thoughts on the center of both of your palms. As you inhale, imagine an energy traveling from the base of your spine and merging at your heart. As the energy enters your heart, allow the energy to travel down your arms and release through both of your palms when you exhale.

4. *Cup your hands:* Create a cup with both of your hands by touching the tips of your index fingers with the tips of your thumbs. Align the rest of your fingertips with the tips of your index fingers. Your hands should look like a cup you can drink water with. Cupping your hands in this manner will allow the energy being released through your hands to accumulate and focus like a laser.

5. *Prayer of intention:* Place your cupped hands on your lap, palms upward, and say a prayer. Ask God and your guides to help you use your hands, mind, and intuition to sense and detect any injury or illness in the human body.

6. *Self-check:* To check the flow of energy in your hands, place your cupped hands over your chest. Close your eyes and feel the energy from your hands. What is the energy being pulled toward? How strong is this energy today? Did any mental pictures of any part of your body enter your mind? If so, move your hand to that spot and see if you can determine what is going on inside of you.

7. *Reading the ha of your own body:* Take the time to identify any unusual feelings or hunches you may have while doing this self-assessment. Some of your personal readings should not surprise you, only confirming what you already know about your conditions. When you have completed this self-check, you are ready to conduct the first of two different scans on another person.

8. *Using your hands to read the ha of another person:* You should have performed all the steps listed above before working on another person. Before reading the ha of another person, be sure you ask their permission. This permission should include the specific area your client is concerned about. Limit your scan based on their request.

9. *Scanning your client:* To perform the scan, place your cupped hands directly over the area under investigation. You do not need to make physical contact with your client's body. Close your eyes, feel your hands, and be aware of any images you may receive regarding the area. As you receive this information, write these impressions down on a piece of paper or use a variation of my worksheet found at the end of this chapter. There are two different scans you will be performing: 1) a Ha scan, which helps you locate the pain or injury, and 2) the Ki'i scan, which involves describing what is physically happening below the skin's surface, hidden from view.

Protocols

The Ha Scan

We will now be working with our hands to detect the flow of energy and locate and describe any illness or injury in the human body. The purpose of the Ha Scan is to read the flow of energy in the human body to locate the specific spot where the injury is. Notice where the energy from your hand is pulling toward and how strong the pull is. Move your hands to the areas pulling the strongest. Besides location, we are also attempting to learn the level of pain in the area, as well as the injury or illness' possible causes and current condition. This information can be gathered by reading the ha energy correctly.

To help you with the scan, you will need a proxy sketch of the human body like the worksheet at the end of this chapter. You may copy the form as needed. As you receive details regarding the location and nature of this injury or illness, log your findings on your proxy sketch. I use circles marked in pink to indicate trouble spots on the body, and written notes to write the impressions I receive regarding the hot spots. Your Ha Scan is your "first impressions" of your client's physical condition.

The Ki'i Scan

The Ki'i Scan is done after you identify all the hot spots that pulled energy in your client's body. The Ki'i Scan can be done on your client or using the proxy sketch.

Before doing the Ki'i Scan, your mind needs to be in the right place. You must believe you can see or sense what is happening in the spots you identified. It is not necessary for you to know the exact medical term for the area you are looking at. It is okay to describe what you see or sense in terms you understand. As you begin to work with other professionals in the medical field, it will be helpful to familiarize yourself with human anatomy and its correct terms.

As you approach each of the hot spots you identified on the proxy, relax, and tell yourself, "Show me what is happening here." Remember, the human body is made of several layers, so you may need to imagine going through each layer before you arrive at the trouble spot.

Open yourself to receiving any images or impressions from this area, noting how deep this injury is and what body structure may be involved. Write or draw your impressions next to the area marked on the proxy.

Reporting your findings

Once your scans are completed, you may report your findings to your client. It is important that you remind your clients you are not a medical doctor and cannot make any diagnosis on any condition you observed. You are limited to describing what you sensed and saw, nothing more. It is okay to advise your client to see a medical doctor if you think it will be helpful for their condition. Do not offer any remedies, such as herbs, tonics, or exercises.

Sometimes, your client will want a copy of your worksheet, so be sure you avoid making any medical conclusion on your proxy sheet or notes. If your client plans to visit a doctor, find out when and schedule a callback after the doctor visit. This follow-up will help you get feedback on the work you did, including what you got correct and any issue you may have missed.

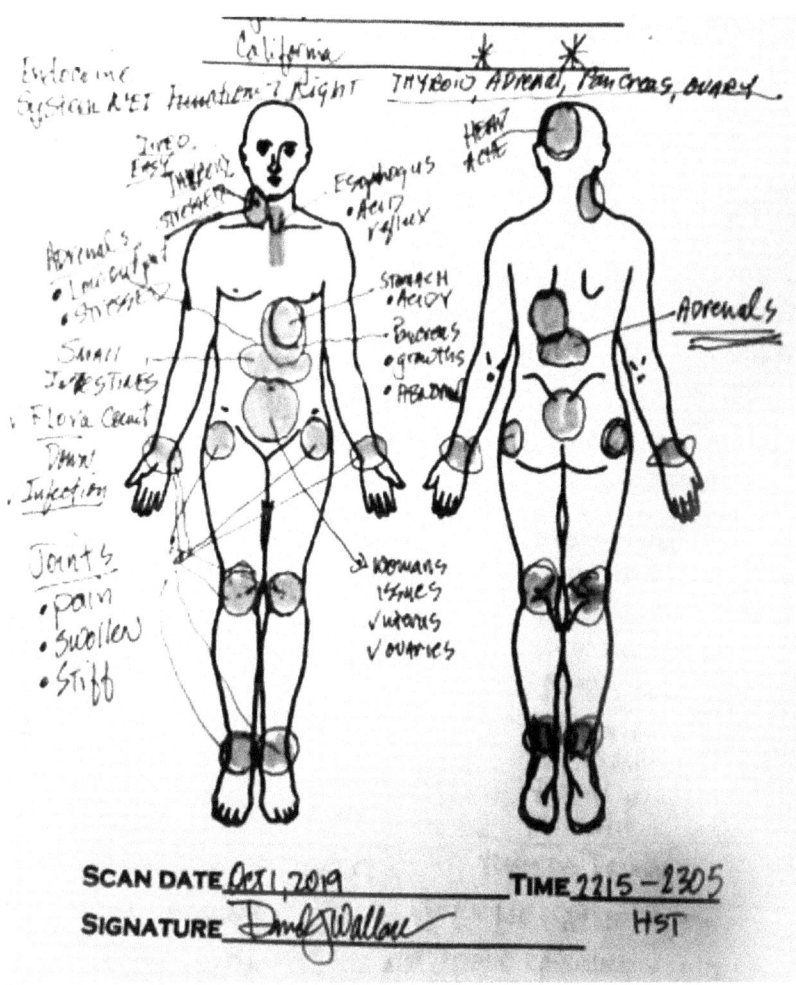

Sample of proxy worksheet for a health scan I completed. The highlighted areas are the areas that pulled energy during my scan. This scan was completed remotely because my client was in California at the time.

Summary

In this chapter, I shared a glimpse of the Ha Ki'i Method of Medical Intuition I have developed and use in my healing practice. The set of instructions is a work in progress that needs further development and refining.

Exercise

Form a cup with your hand by touching your thumbs with the tips of your index fingers. Then curl the rest of your fingers so the tips of all your fingers are aligned with the tip of your index finger. Place your cupped hands palms up on your lap and close your eyes. Imagine a powerful ball of light appearing in the middle of your palms. Feel the warmth from this energy. Count to twenty. Then place your cupped palms over your chest covering your heart. Hold your hands in place for at least five minutes. When done, in the space below, describe what you felt or saw after placing your palms on your chest.

_____

_____

_____

_____

_____

_____

_____

_____

_____

Client Name _____

Address _____

_____

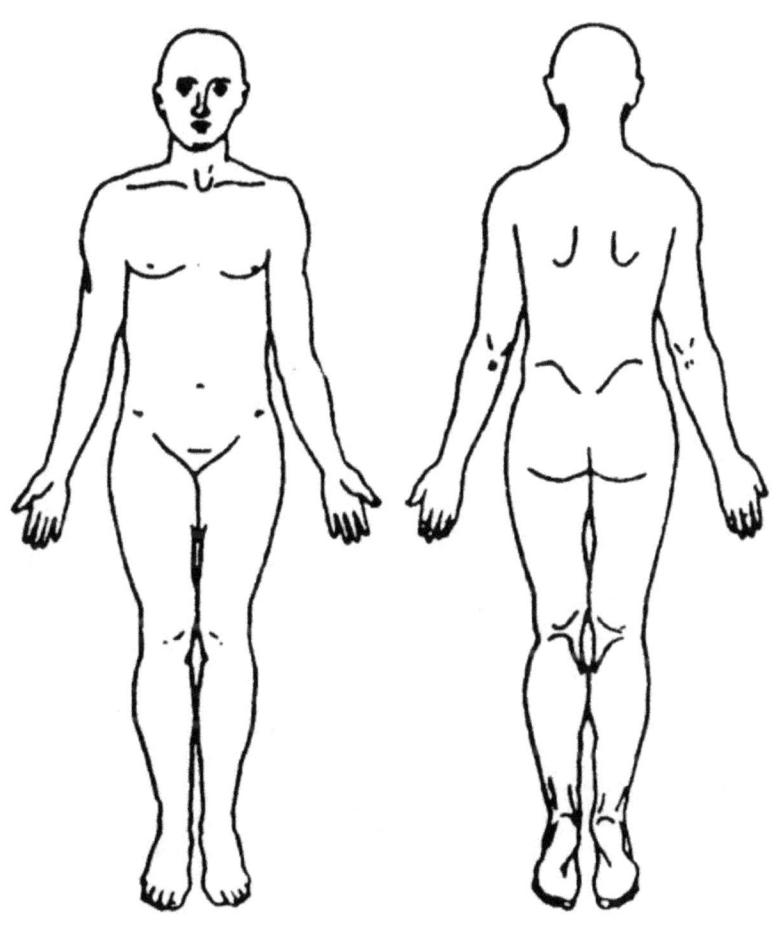

Scan Date _____ **Time** _____

Signature _____

CHAPTER 14
PREDICTING YOUR FUTURE

> "The first thing you need to learn is that an Oracle must choose very carefully how they influence the future. Sometimes a tiny ripple in the now can cause a huge drift. The future is never set, you see, it changes with every choice we make. And changing the larger currents of Fate, even by accident, comes at a heavy price."
>
> — Gwen Mitchell, *Rain of Ash*

In the last chapter, we examined the Ha Ki'i Method of Medical Intuition and my work as a medical intuitive. In this chapter, I will describe a method I use to make predictions on sporting events such as the NFL, CFL, NBA, and WNBA. This is taken from my training manual I use in my Picking Winner$ workshops.

What would you do if you had the ability to accurately predict the future? How would you use this ability? What events would you focus on? How could you benefit from this ability? These are some issues you need to consider when you learn the Associative Remote Viewing (ARV) method you will be exploring in this chapter.

Accurately predicting the future is extremely difficult no matter how talented you are. Achieving and maintaining a 100 percent accuracy rate is highly unlikely. However, that does not mean you should stop trying since in gambling, you only need to be 51 percent accurate to be in the money. Predicting future outcomes is not just limited to gambling; it could also be used in stocks, commodities, and money markets. It can also help you make important decisions based on your desired outcome.

People around the world use many tools to make predictions. These include tarot cards, dowsing pendulums, automatic writing, runes, crystal balls, and lucid dreaming or visions. The tool I have been using to make predictions on professional sports and stocks for more than ten years is Associative Remote Viewing.

What is ARV and how does it work?

Debra Lyn Katz, founder of the International School of Clairvoyance, describes Associative Remote Viewing as "a methodology utilized primarily for predicting the result of events, where there are two or more possible outcomes."

ARV works with associations we create between the events we want to examine, their possible outcomes, and target photos or sketches that represent the possible outcomes. For example, in a sporting event, one of the possible outcomes you can examine is the point total, commonly referred to as the over/under. The total score for a game can either go over or remain under a certain number of points.

To work this part of the game, you will need a target that represents the over and another target representing the under. We then create a sketch based on the perceptions we receive from our target photos. Our prediction for this game is based on how well we describe one of the target photos. If our sketches or impressions match the photo representing the over, then our prediction is over. You will find an example of an ARV session later in this chapter.

PREDICTING YOUR FUTURE 197

Why sports?

To become proficient at a skill requires practice and repetition. To practice, there must be opportunity. Sports provide us with that opportunity since there is a sporting event occurring every day of the week. As you are learning this skill, it is important to work a wide variety of sports until you identify the specific sports you read well and the ones you do poorly at. Several sports overlap each other, especially during the summer months. Take advantage of these time periods to see if you can broaden your choices. The more choices you have, the more games you can work.

The ARV packet

I designed an ARV packet to help us make predictions on games or any events that may involve two possible outcomes. The instructions that follow will help you get started on making predictions on sporting events or the rise and fall of stock prices.

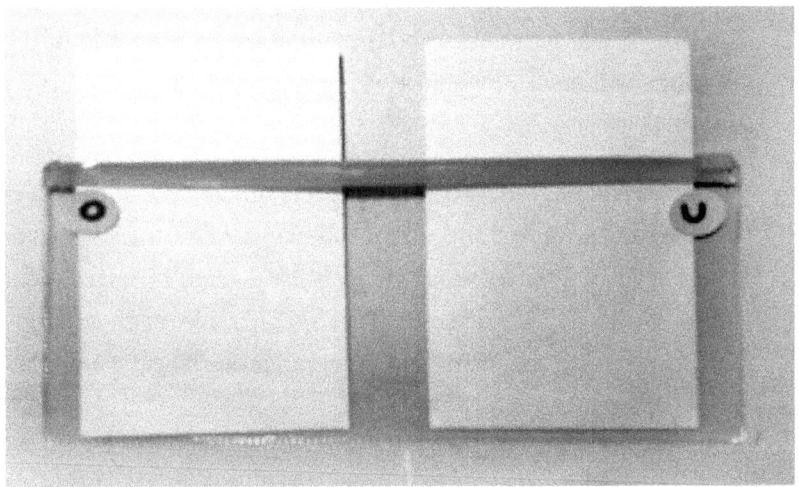

ARV packet, Over and Under showing with envelopes ready for reading

Materials needed:

1. Zip-up envelope

   The first component to the ARV Packet is the zip-up envelope. Any zip-up envelope that is at least 9½ inches long and 5 inches tall will do. Some of the zip-up envelopes I have used in the past are bank deposit envelopes and envelopes used for school supplies. Check out the stationary department at your local drugstore or Walmart.

2. Stickers

   On the outside top corners of the zip-up envelope, you will find four circular stickers with the letters O, U, F, and D written on them. Notice that the stickers are placed in the corners of the zip-up envelope, just below the zipper.

   On the first side of your envelope, using a Sharpie, mark the left sticker with the letter F. The letter F represents FAVORITE. Go to the sticker to the right corner of the envelope and mark it with the letter D. D represents DOG, or underdog. This side of the envelope will be used when working the point spread or money line of a game.

   Now that you have marked both stickers on one side of the envelope, flip the envelope and do the following: Mark the left sticker with the letter O. O represents OVER. Now mark the right sticker with the letter U. U represents Under. This side of the envelope will be used when working the over/under of a game.

3. Ten envelopes

   The next component of your ARV packet is ten envelopes. The best type of envelope to use is a standard size envelope with a security feature that prevents you from seeing the envelope's contents. Make sure the envelopes are clean, no markings on them.

4. Ten photos

    The most important component of your ARV packet is the ten photos you will be selecting as your initial target photos. If you want to use the same images I use in my packet, you may order a completely assembled ARV packet from my website: www.IntuitiveInsightsHawaii.com.

    You can obtain your ten target photos in many ways. One option is to do an image search on the internet of topics that interest you. An option I use is cutting out photos from old *National Geographic* magazines. These magazines are available at your local library when the magazines are recycled.

    When selecting your ten target photos, several things must be considered. 1) Select photos that are meaningful to you. A meaningful photo will communicate better with you. 2) Select photos that are active. Movement, emotions, and activity carry their own energy. 3) Select photos that are different from each other. Avoid choosing photos that are similar in nature since they can blend and confuse your readings.

    As you begin to use your target photos, do not hesitate to replace photos that do not communicate with you. You may want to rotate photos to avoid stale readings.

    Once you collect your ten photos, cut them into similar sizes; then place them into individual envelopes. *Do not seal the envelopes.* You now have your first set of target photos for making your ARV predictions.

Steno pad

The second component to your ARV toolset is a steno pad. Steno pads can be purchased in bulk from Walmart for about $1 each during back to school sales. Stock up on these when you can.

This is how you will set up your steno pad to work the over, under, and point spread for a sporting event. Turn to a new page in your steno pad and copy the form displayed above onto this new page. Below, each of the headings marked on the steno pad will be explained in detail.

```
NFL              NFL1901-A    5 SepT 19
              PACKERS/BEARS
                   O/U 46

SKETCH                    F13




Sound Smell Taste Tex    Temp    Sight




O:                        U:

Prediction               Outcome
```

Admin Section

The Admin Section is the top section of the form that contains three items. To the very top left of the sheet is the sport or league you are working. In the example, the league listed is the NFL (National Football League).

In the center of the Admin Section is the Game ID number. The Game ID number can be a random set of numbers and letters. I use my ID numbers to track the league I am working, the year, and the game number. Below the Game ID number are the names of the teams playing the game. Below that is the game line you will be working. In the example, the Game ID number is NFL1901-A. The teams playing are the Packers and the Bears. The game line we are working is the over/under which was posted at 46 points.

The final item making up the Admin Section is the date of the event located in the top right corner of the form. The date for the game is September 5, 2019. The Admin Section identifies the sport, teams, game line, and date of the game you will be working. A line below this information separates this section from the rest of the worksheet.

Sketch

The next section of the form below the Admin Section is the Sketch Box. This is where you will be drawing or describing your initial impressions for your readings. All your initial sensing of the target should be drawn or written in this space.

FB

The FB (feedback) is the box to the right of the Sketch Box where you will be drawing your feedback sketch once the game has finished. In this space, you will create a sketch associated with the game's winning outcome. Whether or not your initial sketch was correct, you still need to complete this feedback sketch to create your time loop.

Sensory Box

This area is below the Sketch and FB section. The Sensory Box is where you will be recording any extra data you may be picking up from the target. You will probe your sketch for sounds, smell/taste, temperature, textures, and a second sight. Record any findings in this area.

O/U and F/D Descriptors

The next section of the format is reserved for identifying the photos in the first and second envelopes. If you are working the over/under for the games, write the descriptions of the first (O) envelope you open, then the description of the second (U) in their proper places. If you are working the point spread of the game, write the descriptor for the (F) and then the description for the (D). After logging down descriptions and comparing the photos with the sketch you created, you will need to decide which photo matches your sketch. If your sketch does not match either photo, your prediction would be a PASS or NO PLAY.

Prediction

With the O/U and F/D set up on the ARV packet, it will be obvious what your prediction should be. If your sketch does not match photos in either envelope, your prediction will be a PASS or NO PLAY.

Outcome

Here is where you will log the game's results.

Notes

The notes section is for you to log any observations you made regarding the reads you made, what worked, and what you missed. This is an extremely helpful way to learn more about yourself and how you are progressing in ARV.

Now that you have your ARV Packet and your steno pad, we are ready to work our first game. Before working a game, we need to know where to find our game lines for the sport we are interested in.

Where do you find the game lines?

To find the game lines, I use VegasInsider.com. This service will provide you with the latest betting lines from the major sportsbooks in Las Vegas as well as online options. Sportsbooks are organizations that accept bets on sporting events. Westgate Superbook, William Hill, and Circa Sports are popular sportsbooks. VegasInsider.com will list the over/under, point spread, and money line for most of the sports played around the world. Familiarize yourself with reading the game lines so you understand what the lines mean.

Log on to VegasInsider.com. Examine the menu bar that lists the different sports that the site tracks. Click on the sport of your choice. When the sport appears, find the ODDS button just below the main menu bar. Rest your cursor on the ODDS button and click on Vegas odds. The lines for the sports you selected will appear.

READING THE GAME LINES

09/05 8:20 PM	-	-	-	-	-	-	-	-
451 Green Bay	46u-10	46u-10	45½u-10	46u-10	45½u-10	46u-10	46u-10	46u-10	46u-10
452 Chicago	-3½ -10	-3½ -10	-3½ -10	-4 -10	-3½ -10	-3½ -10	-3½ -10	-3½ -10	-4 -10

NFL game line for Packers v Bears on September 5, 2019 as listed on VegasInsider.com

The graphic above shows the game lines for the NFL game to be played on September 5, 2019 at 8:20 p.m. between Green Bay (visitors) and Chicago (home team) as posted on VegasInsider.com. The team listed at the top is always the visitors while the team on the bottom is always the home team.

To the left of the teams are numbers 451 next to Green Bay and 452 next to Chicago. These numbers are needed when making a bet at a sportsbook. The number 451 is for betting the over/under for this game while 452 is for betting the point spread with either Chicago covering or Green Bay covering.

You will then notice to the right of the teams a series of numbers. The numbers 46u -10 are the over/under for the game. The final combined score for this game is expected to remain under 46 points. The -10 means you will need to bet $110 to win $100 if you bet under 46 points.

Below the over/under is the point spread showing -3½ -10. Notice that it is written to the side of Chicago. This means Chicago is favored in this game by 3½ points. If you bet Chicago -3½, you will need to bet $110 to win $100.

The information gathered from Vegas Insider will help you work the two lines of the game, the over/under and the point spread. The lines will change the closer it comes to game time and wagers are placed. It is important to track the lines at the time of your posted bets.

Now that you have your ARV packet and your steno pad, and you know where to find your game lines for the sport of your choice, we are ready to work our first game.

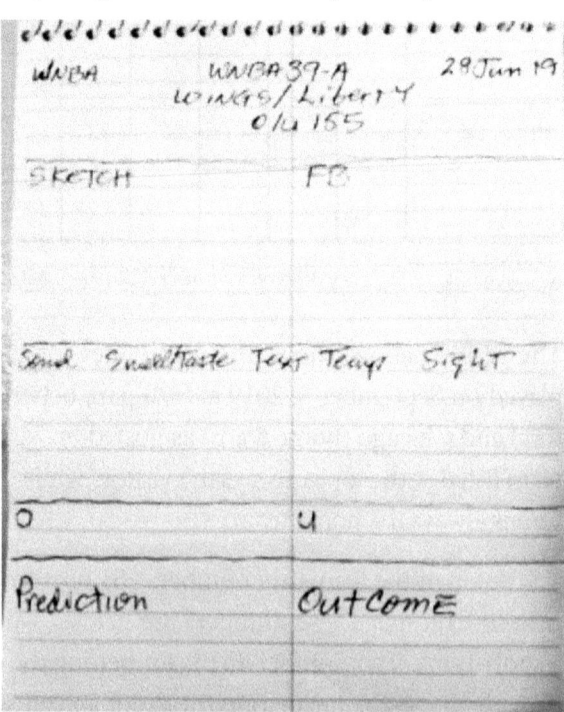

Over/under format for WNBA game

Practice game

The game you will be working is the WNBA game played on June 28, 2019 between the Wings and Liberty. The over/under for this game was 155 points. Set up your steno pad as shown on previous page.

Organize

Get all the supplies you need: ARV packet, steno pad, and pen. Select a quiet place to do your work.

Cool down

Cool down will take about fifteen to twenty minutes. During this time, calm your mind through meditation, controlled breathing, or listening to soothing music. Cool down is used to calm yourself and relax before you begin your ARV work. ARV and RV work better when you are calm and relaxed.

Get your ARV packet

Turn your zip-up envelope so the stickers with the O and U are facing upward.

Remove all ten envelopes from your ARV packet and begin shuffling them. While shuffling the photos, remind yourself that you are working the WNBA game between the Wings and Liberty played on June 28, 2019 and the over/under was 155. Ask the photos in the envelope to communicate the truth to you regarding the game's outcome.

Randomly select one envelope

After selecting your first envelope, hold it in front of you and say, "Describe the photo in this envelope if the final combined score at the end of the game goes over 155 points." Place the envelope, lengthwise up, behind the O sticker. (See image on page 197)

Randomly select another envelope

After selecting your second envelope, hold it in front of you and say, "Describe the photo in this envelope if the final combined score at the end of the game remains under 155 points." Place the envelope, lengthwise up, behind the U sticker.

Relax and clear your mind for five minutes

Relax and clear your mind for five minutes. During this time, tell yourself, "Show me the photo I need to see."

Turn your attention to FB space

When ready, focus on the FB Box next to the Sketch Box. Tell yourself, "Show me the sketch I will be drawing here during feedback." Close your eyes, tilt your head back, and wait for an image to appear.

Create your sketch

After receiving your impressions in your mind's eye, create a sketch that matches one of the ten target photos that best matches your visual image. Do this quickly.

Complete sensory box

Every target photo you choose will have extra data that is part of the target that will come across in your reading. This data includes sounds, smells, tastes, temperatures, textures, and a second visual. Take time to fill this out to get a better understanding of what you are seeing and feeling regarding the target photo.

Open envelope O

Look at the photo assigned to O. Describe it in the spot designated O. Compare it to the sketch you created. How well does your sketch match your photo?

Open envelope U

Look at the photo assigned to U. Describe it in the spot designated U. Compare it to the sketch you created. How well does your sketch match your photo?

Compare both photos against your sketch

Decide which photo matches your sketch the best. If photo O matches your sketch, then your prediction will be over 155 points. If photo U matches your sketch, then your prediction will be under 155 points.

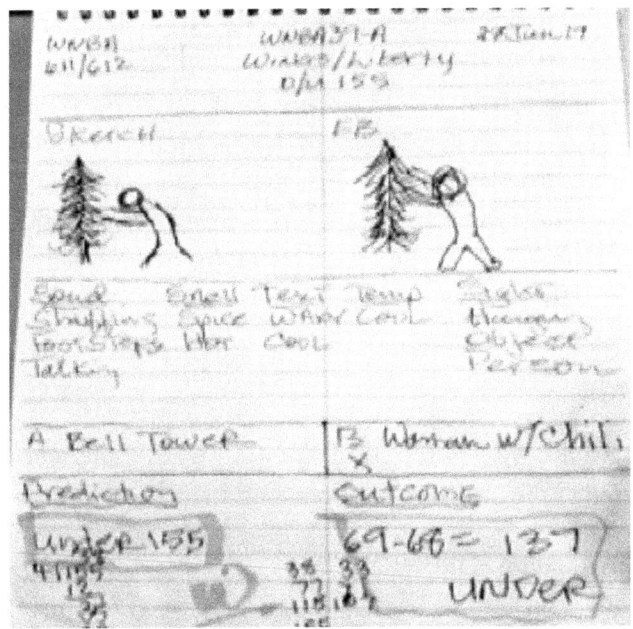

Actual worksheet for game

Outcome of the game

The final score of this game was 69-68 for a combined score of 137. The correct outcome was under. The photo for U is the correct image for this part of the game.

Feedback

To close your time loop, we must now create our feedback sketch with the correct image. If you got this correct, congratulations. If not, do not worry about it. This is your first application of this method. Since we are using different sets of photos, please draw the correct image in the Feedback section based on the photos you used.

Working the point spread

To work the point spread of a game, use the same format and the processes you used to make the over/under reading. The only changes you will need to make are in the top administrative section, where you will write the point spread and favored team under the names of the two teams playing. You will also need to flip your ARV packet to the side where the F and D stickers are. From that point, you just repeat the same process you used to work the over/under.

Summary

In this chapter, you were introduced to the ARV method I use to make predictions on sporting events and stocks. If you have gone through the process to create your own ARV packet, you are now equipped to make predictions of your own. If you need help or have questions about this section, feel free to contact me at (808) 349-4788. Good luck and have fun!

Exercise

Once you have assembled your ARV packet, what sport or event will you use it for? How do you expect it to work for you over time?

CHAPTER 15

LIVING AS A KAHU AND PSYCHIC

"People need hard times and oppression to develop psychic muscles."

— Emily Dickinson

In the last chapter, you were introduced to the ARV method I use to make predictions on sporting events. You were invited to assemble your ARV packet and practice the process I have been using successfully for several years. In this chapter, we will explore my work as a kahu and psychic counselor.

What is a kahu? Is a kahu a kahuna? Does a kahu have to be religiously affiliated? These questions are often asked by my clients, so in this chapter, I will be explaining my role as a kahu.

A kahu is a steward or caretaker. Every kahu has taken on a certain *kuleana* (area of responsibility). That kuleana defines the type of kahu a person is. For example, a person responsible for taking care of a park or a piece of land is a *kahu aina* (steward of the land). Some kahu decide to be affiliated with a religion, taking upon themselves the role of pastor or reverend, while others like me decide to take on the responsibility of healing and teaching. If you are currently working in a field to which you are totally committed, you would qualify as a kahu.

Kahu are not kahuna. To become a kahuna, you must be trained by a kahuna. Just because your ancestors were kahuna does not mean you are also a kahuna, although you may have inherited some spiritual powers and gifts from your ancestors. The only hereditary kahuna I am familiar with is the Kahuna Nui, who are descendants of Pa'ao, the first Kahuna Nui from Tahiti. Currently, several Native Hawaiian schools are training modern kahuna in the fields of healing, self-defense, building, *uhi* (tattoo), and various art forms.

Describing my stewardship

My work as a kahu covers three areas: healing, teaching, and psychic counseling. My healing practice is embodied in the Ha Ki'i Healing and Medical Intuition protocols I described in previous chapters. As a medical intuitive, I help people understand what is happening to their bodies so they can accept and receive the proper care they may need to heal. Ha Ki'i Healing allows me to direct healing toward my clients who are ill so they can recover faster. Finally, as a psychic counselor, I help guide and counsel people to make the best choices in their lives so they can live happy and productive lives.

Many levels to healing exist, and while most healing methods focus on healing the physical, healing on the mental, emotional, and spiritual planes is also necessary.

Bridging the spiritual and physical gap

As a kahu, numerous people have asked me to help explain and resolve issues that often defy logic. Many of these situations involve an unhappy spirit who is bothering an individual or family. Some situations are created by a person who refuses to accept what seems obvious to practitioners like me. My role in these situations is to help people bridge the gap between themselves and the spirit world so their fears and anxieties can be peacefully resolved. Here are two examples from my practice to illustrate how to bridge the gap.

The angry fetus

This incident was brought to my attention by one of my former coworkers on Tuesday, March 8, 2016. One of our mutual friends, whom I will call Angie, had been experiencing something very unusual. Red marks were mysteriously appearing on the backs of Angie's arms. At first, she thought these marks were the hives, but when others examined them, they appeared to be long, narrow scratches. The scratches would appear while Angie was home, while she was sleeping, and while she was at work. Angie was even scratched while visiting her mother-in-law. The frequency of these scratching attacks appeared to be on the rise, starting off with two to three per day, to more than eight within the days before I saw her. After learning Angie was being scratched at multiple locations, it became obvious to me that whatever was causing the scratches was not attached to a specific place; it was attached to her.

By the time I was contacted, Angie had been enduring these scratches for about two weeks.

When Angie called me, I got her permission to project my consciousness to view what was causing the scratches. I sensed that a small orb of energy had attached itself to the small of Angie's back. The first impression I got was "fetus." For some reason, this orb was angry and venting its frustrations on Angie. After verifying what I saw, I called Angie to collect more information and ask her some important questions.

My first question was "Have you had any miscarriages in the past few months?"

She told me she had had two miscarriages in the last three to five months beginning in late 2015. I asked her if any of these miscarriages was unusual. Angie told me the last miscarriage was unusual because she had tried to keep it a secret from her husband. When her doctor did a scan, a developing fetus appeared to be in her. A few weeks later, when she took her husband with her for her second checkup, the fetus was no longer there. After hearing this, I realized we were dealing with a miscarried fetus who had some issues with mom. To be certain I was dealing with a fetus, I went through all my questions to ensure no one was angry with Angie, or jealous of her, and that she had not visited a sacred site.

My focus was now turned to mom and a miscarried fetus. Why was this fetus angry at mom? When I informed Angie of my impressions, she went silent. I then asked her what had happened with her and her husband just weeks before the scratching began to appear. Angie dropped a bombshell. A few days before the scratches began to appear, Angie and her husband had decided to stop trying to get pregnant again. They already had two sons, and since Angie was getting older, she did not want to risk having a child born with a handicap.

As Angie poured her heart out to me, I looked out of my workstation window and saw a cloud formation south of me. The cloud appeared to be a fetus, curled up in its mother's womb. As the wind carried this cloud west, it morphed into a ballerina in a tutu, with her arms arced over her head. It was a clear indication to me that this fetus was a little girl. This little girl was angry with her mom for stopping short of bringing her into this world. This made perfect sense to me and Angie.

As I looked for a solution to this situation, I felt urged to suggest the following plan to help mother and daughter come to a peaceful resolution.

Step one was for Angie to ask forgiveness from her child's spirit. Step two was to give the child a name because if this child remained nameless, and unclaimed, its spirit would be left in limbo, possibly joining the ranks of the Lapu lapu kolohe (roaming ghosts). I asked Angie to find a suitable name for her daughter and to claim this child as hers, making her part of the family. This would give the child's spirit access to the 'aumakua and kupuna (ancestors) who would guide her to where she needed to go. The final step was a cleansing in the ocean to wash away the attachment's residual effects. During this cleansing, Angie needed to forgive herself for the decisions she had made that led to the attachment.

Angie followed my instructions, and by Thursday, March 10, 2016, she had completed all three steps. The scratching episodes stopped on Wednesday evening, after Angie apologized to the spirit of the child and gave her a name. The scratches never appeared again.

Dying in a strange land

In June 2016, I received a call from a woman I will call Martha, who would be flying in from California to meet with several healers here in Hawaii. Martha was under the impression that the healers in Hawaii were the only ones who could help her with her condition, which she did not want to discuss with me over the phone. As I spoke with her, I could sense she was extremely ill and possibly terminal. Her light was fading fast. I arranged for a face-to-face meeting with Martha and her husband Jay at the Keaiwa Heiau in Aiea. Keaiwa Heiau was part of a larger ancient healing center that reached high into the Ko'olau mountain range and into Pearl Harbor. Healing herbs can be found in every biome in the diverse terrain surrounding Keaiwa. This is where I prefer to meet people who are terribly ill.

On the appointed day and time, I arrived early at Keaiwa and prepared to meet Martha and Jay by clearing and cleansing the pavilion closest to the heiau. When Martha and Jay drove in to the Heiau grounds, I could feel a shift in the energy. As Martha got out of the car, aided by Jay, I could see that Martha was worn, tired, and physically weak. She was also surrounded by a host of spirits who stuck awfully close to her. These spirits were her ancestors who were there to guide her to the next dimension. Their presence was an indication that Martha's time on earth was nearing its end.

By the time Martha arrived at the pavilion, based on my physical reaction toward her presence, I knew she had cancer. I did a quick scan of Martha's body to understand what I was dealing with. The cancer had spread from her breast into her lymph system and was now in every major organ in her body, killing her.

"Aloha, Kahu Dave," said Martha. "Thank you for meeting with me and Jay today."

"You are most welcome, Martha," I replied, "How can I help you today?"

Martha's eyes teared up and she began to sob.

"Don't worry, Martha. I know why you are here."

Martha sobbed even more as Jay gave me a surprised look.

"I know you have cancer, and it has invaded your entire system. This cancer is causing your organs to shut down. You are here in Hawaii looking for a miracle cure since medical doctors have been unable to help you. Is that right?"

A sobbing Martha shook her head "Yes."

"We've seen several healers so far, and they have told us that things should be improving soon," inserted Jay, attempting to raise Martha's spirits.

"If that is what you believe, then why are you here today?"

There was an uncomfortable silence.

"Martha, Jay, your visit with me today is to discover the truth. If you are seeking the truth, I will share with you my observations, and following that, you will need to make an important choice. Are both of you ready for the truth?"

"And what choice would that be, Kahu?" asked Jay.

"The choice Martha needs to make is whether she wants to die in a strange land, surrounded by strangers, or die while surrounded by her family, friends, and loved ones in a place she knows and loves."

Jay slammed his hands on the table.

"This is bullshit!" shouted Jay.

Martha stroked Jay's neck to calm him down.

"It's okay, dear. Let us hear what Kahu has to say."

I paused until I was assured everyone's emotions were under control.

"Mahalo, Martha. Let me explain some of the things I see around you."

I described the multitude of spirits that had assembled around Martha. As I began describing them, Martha confirmed their identities. They were her parents, grandparents, aunts, and uncles who had passed on.

"Why are my family members surrounding me at this time?" she asked.

"Before I answer that," I replied, "I have a question for you. Have you been seeing any of these family members or special friends that have passed on?"

Martha smiled.

"Yes, I have."

"Who have you seen, and what has this person been saying to you?"

Martha told me she had been seeing a childhood friend who had died several years ago. She and this friend had been inseparable as children and young adults. They went to the same schools, lived near each other, and attended the same church. This friend, who had died in a tragic accident, had been visiting Martha off and on for the last couple of weeks. Lately, Martha's friend has been asking her to follow her, but Martha had been afraid.

"Your friend and family members are here to help you make the transition to heaven," I told her.

"Do you know what heaven looks and feels like, Kahu?" asked a concerned Martha.

"Yes; in fact, I was given a view of heaven when I was in my thirties."

I proceeded to describe my second NDE where I was given a glimpse of heaven through the end of a long, crooked tunnel. I shared the amazing feeling of love, forgiveness, and fulfillment that is overwhelming from a mortal's perspective. Martha and Jay listened intently as tears poured down their faces. When I finished describing my NDE, Jay calmly asked, "So Kahu Dave, what should we do?"

"Well, you have a choice to make. You can stay here and continue to see the rest of the healers you have made appointments with, but if you do that, your wife will probably die here in Hawaii, surrounded by a bunch of strangers, in a place she has no attachment to. The other choice is to return home as soon as possible and contact all your loved ones. There are those you need to mend relationships with, mainly for their sake. When the time comes, Martha will be surrounded by her loved ones, and she will die in a place she knows and loves. Martha's time is remarkably close."

With that, I closed the session with a prayer. We hugged and went our separate ways.

Later that night, Jay called me to say he and Martha were heading back to California. Jay and Martha had met with me on a Tuesday. They left Hawaii the following day and arrived in California Wednesday evening. Two days later, on Friday, Jay called to inform me that Martha had died. They had contacted their children, brothers, sisters, and other family members, and Martha had made the peaceful transition in her home of thirty years surrounded by her loved ones. Being able to be with her family at this point in her life brought comfort and healing to Martha, Jay, and her entire family. They came to Hawaii looking for a miracle. That miracle was the healing of their family.

People problem, not spiritual problem

Would you build your home in a former cemetery if the land were cheap enough? Would you accept topsoil for your home from a cemetery? What would be the consequences if you did?

I have seen the consequences of these actions myself. Below are some incidents I have witnessed.

Campbell High Football Field

When Campbell High School built its football stadium, it needed a lot of topsoil to do it. One contractor hired to create the field found a source of cheap topsoil from a local cemetery. The new stadium was beautiful, but almost immediately after opening, many of the athletes began having strange injuries and illnesses while playing on the field. When the source of the topsoil was revealed, the field was blessed by a priest, but the problem continued. Over the years, the field has been blessed several times, but nothing has changed. The field continues to plague the athletes to this day.

Ewa Beach

Campbell High School is built in Ewa Beach, in an area known as Puuloa by ancient Hawaiians. The ancient Hawaiians recognized that not all spirits of deceased loved ones make the transition to the next world. Some remain on this plane and refuse to go. Because of this, Hawaiians reserved areas on each island for these villages of the dead so these spirits could have a home. Such areas on Oahu include present-day Puuloa, Ewa Beach, Ewa, and Kapolei. The old Hawaiians left these places barren, so the spirits claimed them. Since land is at a premium on Oahu, these lands belonging to the dead have come under attack. These barren lands are now cluttered with homes. These new homes have problems between their human owners and the spirits who were there first. Most of my calls for these types of problems come from new developments in these places such as Ocean Point and Hoakalei. These are the newer developments in the area.

Since spirits have claimed these areas for hundreds of years, many of these spirits are upset with humans who are now encroaching onto their territories. Not all spirits will fight back, but those who do can be very nasty and stubborn.

Unhappy stones

One interesting case I was called to investigate involved a family who lived in Ocean Pointe in Ewa Beach. They had recently moved into a ground floor condo and were being bothered by something pounding on their back door and wall late at night.

After getting the family's permission, I paid an "astral" visit to their home. An astral visit involves me projecting my *astral body* (a subtle body often referred to as the dream body) to my client's home rather than doing a remote viewing session. To me, the astral plane is more alive, containing more energy than the physical plane. It is easier for me to sense what is happening in the home. Many times, what I see on this plane is more metaphoric than real. Common objects can become animated, and openly communicate with me. This helps me zero in on the problems my clients face.

In my astral form, I went to the back door, which was a sliding door leading to the backyard. In the backyard was a pile of river stones. I saw one of the stones roll off the stack and smack into the back wall of the house, making a loud BANG! The stone then rolled back to the pile. I approached the stones and asked them why they were unhappy. I was given a short vision of how these stones were part of an ancient Hawaiian house foundation that had disintegrated. Several of the stones wanted to be returned to where they had been picked up. The person who took the stones did not ask their permission and did not follow gathering protocols. A couple of the stones in the pile were okay with their new location, but six of them wanted to be returned to their previous location. I asked the six disgruntled stones to cluster together on the ground to the right of the stone pile so they could be easily identified.

Now understanding the problem's source, I recalled my astral body, and the next day, I made an appointment with the family. It was clear the family was not aware of the gathering protocols when collecting stones, so I educated them regarding this. We went outside to the pile of stones, and I helped identify the stones that did not want to be there. These stones were then returned to the place where they were gathered. Once the stones were returned, the pounding on the back door and wall stopped.

Psychic counseling

What if you could see people's lives flash before your eyes, like watching a movie on fast forward? Could you use this information to help other people? How reliable are these visions? The legitimacy of this information is a constant consideration when I am performing my psychic counseling.

My counseling sessions are strictly intuitive readings, coming straight from spirit and our ancestors. I do not use tarot cards, playing cards, or dowsing pendulums for my readings. To help me focus on my clients' specific needs, I ask them to limit their scope of my inquiry by coming up with specific questions they want me to look at. By limiting the scope of my inquiry, I can probe the areas relevant to what my client needs. Without these guidelines, their whole life will flash before me, and it will take too much time and energy to sort things out.

Most of my sessions deal with future actions, which can be very tricky since the future is dependent on the decisions we make. The further we investigate the future, the more uncertainty is involved. For that reason, when doing a future probe for my clients, I use the phrase "if things continue unchanged." The more changes we make in our lives, the more our future changes.

One resource I depend upon for near future predictions and outcomes is my ancestors and my client's ancestors. Our ancestors live in a realm where present, past, and future occupy the same space. Consulting with the ancestors about the near future provides my client and me with the insights we need to help us make the best decisions.

To investigate the distant future, my best tool is to remote view a person's timeline. The RV protocols I use take time and patience, and I will do them only upon special request or if my client is planning an event for a specific time.

A quite common request I get from my clients is to remote view their future Las Vegas trips to identify the game, day, or casino where they will win the most money. The trip's duration is normally four to five days. The variables involved in a reading such as this are dates, times, multiple casino games, several casinos, and winning money. In most cases, I will be able to identify two or three specific events during the trip that will occur exactly as I saw it, while some come remarkably close.

For example, in 2014, I was asked to remote view a four-day Las Vegas trip for a mother and daughter. I took three days to complete the inquiry and I made the following recommendations. First, the daughter would be extremely lucky for the first two days of the trip and should play the high limit slot machines during this time. After the first two days, the daughter should stop gambling. Second, the mother should avoid gambling during the first two days of the trip. After that, she would do better playing a machine that looked like the Wheel of Fortune and had a bonus wheel. Third, they should avoid playing in the downtown casinos and focus on casinos near the south end of the Las Vegas strip. Finally, the only way they would make money during the trip was to keep their winnings and know when to stop.

Following their trip, I called mother and daughter to learn how they did. The daughter's first action upon arriving in Las Vegas was jumping on a $5 slot machine. Within ten spins, she won $5,000. Second, on the final day of the trip, the mother won $1,500 on a twenty-five cent Wheel of Fortune slot machine. All their wins occurred in casinos located on the south end of the Las Vegas strip: The Cosmopolitan and New York, New York. Sadly, they did not walk away winners since they spent a lot of time playing with their friends in the downtown casinos, which almost emptied their bankrolls.

Summary

In this chapter, we examined the work I do as a kahu and psychic. These roles are often closely tied together when I am called upon to help others. In both roles, I spend a lot of time teaching others about our culture here in the islands and respecting the places they call home. It is a reminder that we should always be mindful of what we do and where we do it.

Exercise

Do you think spirits' claims to places or objects should be respected? Why or why not?

_____

_____

_____

_____

_____

_____

If you experienced a haunting in your home, or felt any unusual feeling there, who would you call to help the situation? What outcome would you expect?

_____
_____
_____
_____
_____
_____
_____
_____

CHAPTER 16

BEING THE RELUCTANT LEADER

> "Some are born great, some achieve greatness, and some have greatness thrust upon them."
>
> — William Shakespeare

In the previous chapter, we looked at my existing practice as a kahu and psychic counselor. In this final chapter, I will discuss the interesting case of the reluctant leader and how reluctant leaders can be the best people to fill leadership roles.

How many of you think you were destined to lead? How many of you actively pursued leadership roles in school, church, work, sports, or your community? Why do you think you are leadership material? What motivates you to become a leader? How you answer these questions will determine what kind of leader you are.

Not me

I had no desire to become a leader. I was a second son for most of my life, relegated to follower and support roles in my family. In school, racial prejudices and favoritism of the dominant culture reinforced my status as a second-class person. I was not expected to lead and was never given the opportunity to do so. I preferred to blend quietly into the background.

While trying to avoid the limelight and attention that come with being a leader, I found myself in countless situations as a child, teenager, and adult where I became a leader by default. There would be a void in leadership that required someone with a certain skill set to step up and fill the void. Reluctantly, I took the reins when no one else wanted to.

What is a reluctant leader?

Reluctant leaders are people who do not really seek to be leaders. They have some concept of what might happen to them if they step forward and do the right thing, so they pause, but they do it anyway. They are not seeking the limelight. They are not looking for glory. They are doing the right thing despite their own doubts. They are doing the right thing simply because they do not have it in them *not* to try to stand up for what is right and fair, or to lead when there is a need.

Examples of reluctant leaders in history

Moses

When God asked Moses to lead his chosen people from bondage in Egypt, Moses came up with a long list of reasons why God had made a mistake. He did not want to take on that leadership role. Moses realized the tremendous challenges he would be facing. His first challenge was convincing the Egyptian pharaoh to free the Israelites. Once they were freed, Moses could probably anticipate the problems he would face as leader of a nation of freed slaves searching for a homeland of which only God knew the location. The sheer logistics involving food, water shelter, and care for all these people would weigh heavily on a leader's shoulders. Eventually, Moses accepted his role as the Great Deliverer, realizing he was the only person alive who could perform that task. To make up for his shortcomings and weaknesses, he surrounded himself with capable people such as his brother Aaron and Joshua.

Cincinnatus

Cincinnatus was a Roman statesman and general who retired from public service. Despite his old age, he worked his own small farm until an invasion about 458 BC prompted his fellow citizens to call for his leadership. He left his farm to assume complete control over Rome and its legions. Upon achieving a swift victory in a matter of a few short weeks, Cincinnatus surrendered his power and its perquisites and returned to his life as a farmer. His success and immediate resignation of his near-absolute authority has often been cited as an example of outstanding leadership, service to the greater good, civic virtue, humility, and modesty.

My leadership experiences

I will share with you now two examples of my own leadership experiences and how I took on the role of reluctant leader.

Gardening

My first experience as a leader occurred when I was in fourth grade. My teacher, Miss Kosaka, wanted to start a small garden behind our classroom. She had selected a small patch of open ground surrounded by eucalyptus trees. When she told our class her plans, she asked if any of us had experience growing a garden. Several of us raised our hands, including me.

I had been raising my own vegetables in our family garden since I was in kindergarten. I had learned about mulching, using manure, and creating vegetable beds from my dad. In my own garden, I planted radishes, beans, carrots, mustard cabbages, eggplants, cherry tomatoes, and pigeon peas.

One day, Miss Kosaka took all of us to where she envisioned our garden would be and allowed us to poke around in the dirt. I knelt and started feeling the soil's texture. It was the same red clay soil I had in my garden, so I knew how to work this soil. I would need compost and chicken manure. I walked to a spot where the ground felt warm and began to mark out a rectangular area six paces long and three paces wide. My best friend Alex saw what I was doing, so he helped me mark the boundaries by pounding eucalyptus sticks in the ground. Miss Kosaka walked up to me and asked, "David, what are you doing?"

"I am marking the spot for our vegetable bed."

"Why are you doing it here instead of where your other classmates are?" she asked.

"The trees block the sun over there, so the vegetables won't do well there. If we plant over here, the sun will hit the plants from the morning until the late afternoon. That is better for the plants."

Miss Kosaka smiled and instructed the other students to choose spots for their vegetable bed closer to the area I had chosen. As the other students came to where I had set up my bed, I helped them mark the boundaries for their beds, making sure there was room enough between the beds for us to walk. Some listened, but others just ignored me. That did not bother me at all.

After setting up the beds, I asked Miss Kosaka where we would get the tools we needed to turn over the soil. I reminded her that our high school had a farm, so getting picks, shovels, hoes, and water hoses would not be a problem. We just needed to talk to the agriculture teacher. Miss Kosaka did exactly that and secured the right tools for us.

When we finally got our tools, we all went out to work our vegetable beds, four of us to a bed. We took turns turning the soil with the pick, shovel, and hoe until the dirt was loose and free from clumps and stones. As the soil loosened, I scrounged under the trees for rotten tree leaves that were turning to compost. I was able to get a bucketful to take back to my vegetable bed. Some of my classmates saw what I was doing and decided to copy me. As we mixed the compost into the soil, the soil's color changed to a darker tinge. That was what I was looking for.

By the next garden day, I had gathered more compost, which was mixed with chicken manure from our home garden. I placed it in a large rice bag and took it to school. It stunk up the whole classroom. In the days leading up to garden day, my partners and I worked out a plan for our vegetable bed. I suggested we plant radishes and pole beans in alternating rows. I had already experimented with this plan at home, so I knew it would work. My partners agreed to my plans, so I brought my radish and pole bean seeds to school.

At our garden plot, I mixed in about half the bag of compost and manure, building up our vegetable bed. I shared the leftovers with my classmates, who were very appreciative. By this time, several of my classmates were mimicking what my partners and I were doing. I even helped them if they had problems with their beds. My partners and I then marked out about a dozen lines to plant our seeds. I took out my packets of radish seeds and beans and we began sowing our seeds. This caught Miss Kosaka's attention.

"David, why are you folks planting your vegetables so close? And why are you planting two different vegetables? Everyone else is planting just one vegetable in their beds."

"The radishes I am planting grow quickly, so we will have vegetables to eat really soon. By the time we finish harvesting the radishes, the beans will be ready for their poles so they can climb. After a short time, we will get fresh beans. From the same bed, we can get two different crops that will be ready at different times. Otherwise, *poho*, it's a waste of time."

This, coming from a fourth-grade kid, sounded too intelligent, so Miss Kosaka looked skeptical.

"Miss Kosaka, no worry; I did this at home already. It will work."

Sure enough, while many of my classmates were waiting for their broccoli, watermelons, carrots, and tomatoes to mature, our radishes were the first vegetables to be harvested. After the radishes were pulled, I brought in a bundle of tall, skinny branches cut from *haole koa* (Leucaena leucocephala) and my partners and I stuck them into the beds so our beans could have something to climb. In a few weeks, we were harvesting fresh beans.

While growing our garden, my classmates and teacher realized I had some hidden skills useful to the project. While my teacher came up with the idea, she did not have the experience or expertise needed to carry out her vision. From my first day walking the grounds she had selected for our garden, I realized she needed my help. This was my home ground. My own personal garden was only a few blocks away from my classroom. I sensed a void and knew I could help, so I decided to act, rather than asking permission or making a big deal about anything. I carried this skill and reputation over to fifth grade when I became a leader in 4H and specialized in gardening.

SOPU

Another time my skills and talents were needed was when my family and I were living in Utah during the 1980s. I was invited to join the Society of Polynesians in Utah (SOPU). The group's organizers were Samoans, and since I was part Samoan, they wanted me to participate. After attending several meetings, I wanted to sever my ties with them because I felt they lacked a higher purpose than just being a social club.

In 1982, at what I thought would be my final meeting with this group, I voiced my concern about the group's lack of purpose and told the members I wanted to end my ties with them. The group leader then asked me what I would do if I were made the leader of SOPU. I sat back, thought for a few minutes, and then said, "We need to focus on something that will bring Polynesians together for a higher purpose. This organization is only planning fundraisers for parties and trips, but how does that meet the needs of all Polynesians living in Utah? If you keep doing what you are doing, and tapping the same people over and over, you not going to last as an organization."

The room went silent. The leader then asked, "Is there something you see out there that can bring all Polynesians together?"

As soon as he said that, I had a flash of my grandparents, John and Maggie Broad.

"I am not sure, but I have a suggestion," I replied. "How many of you have heard of the Iosepa Colony out in Skull Valley?"

No one had a clue.

"Let me educate you. This colony is in Skull Valley out in Tooele, Utah. It was established by the Mormon Church in the early 1900s to assist the Polynesian converts who had left their island homes and moved to Utah so they could do temple work for their families. My grandparents, John and Maggie Broad, along with several of their family members, lived in Iosepa and had their first two children there, my uncles Edwin and Lionel. Eventually, the colony was disbanded when the Church acquired land in Laie Oahu and built its temple there. My grandparents and many of the Iosepa colonists then moved back to Laie."

"That's a good story," said the leader, "but what is the point?"

"Iosepa was an established colony for several years. Over the years, many of the colonists who died in the colony were buried in a cemetery that is still there in the desert. Since moving to Utah in 1980, my family and I have joined a small group of Hawaiians who spend Memorial Day weekend at the cemetery. We clean the graves on Saturday and work on projects to improve and protect the cemetery. A Hawaiian family chipped in money to buy a fence to surround the graveyard since it sits in the middle of a cattle ranch and the cows were knocking down the grave markers. On Sunday, we have a memorial service; then we have lunch and pack up and leave. If we can organize ourselves and focus our efforts for this Memorial Day event, I am sure it will help attract more Polynesians and bring us together as a people."

A couple of weeks later, I was asked to be the new SOPU chairman. I had my reservations but reluctantly accepted the challenge. I had the vision; now it was up to me to bring that vision to life.

I had almost a year to put together a plan for Memorial Day 1983. I enlisted the talents of my big brother, Bill, who was much more articulate than me and had many connections with other Hawaiian and Polynesian groups around the country. Before moving to Utah to pursue his law degree at BYU, he had been vice president of operations for the Polynesian Cultural Center. While Bill gathered commitments from *hula halau* (hula schools) and entertainers, I worked on the logistics, such as acquiring enough portable toilets and ways to transport them to and from Iosepa. We also needed tents, power, and sound systems since we realized if we did things right, there would be a large crowd. We contacted my uncle Lionel, who was born at Iosepa, and was living in Ogden. He agreed to come and speak at the memorial service. We also got on the radio and spoke about Iosepa as often as possible. We ran newspaper ads and sent invitations to as many people as we could. We stressed that this would be a camping trip in the desert, so people would need to bring food, water, shelter, and appropriate clothing.

On the Friday of Memorial Day weekend, we loaded up our RV rental and my brother drove it to Iosepa. The main celebration was scheduled for Saturday, with a memorial prayer service on Sunday. I rented a large truck from BYU, loaded it up with a dozen portable toilets, and drove to Iosepa. When we arrived at Iosepa, we realized our efforts to bring the Polynesians together had worked. About a hundred people were there already, far more than the usual crowd of twenty to thirty.

I strategically placed the portable toilets around the camping and staging areas while other volunteers helped set up the generator, lights, tents, and sound system. We had toilets, power and lights, sound, and a central meeting place for the activities scheduled for Saturday.

By late Friday evening, our numbers had approached 200 people. We all prepared our meals, had a potluck dinner, and chatted late into the night. All my anxieties left me as I realized every detail I had anticipated and prepared for had resulted in success.

We were blessed with the arrival of my uncle Lionel early the next morning. His arrival marked the beginning of a constant stream of cars with people making their trek to Iosepa. While talking to us, Uncle Lionel pointed to the southwest of the cemetery and told us about some swimming holes in that direction. We decided to transport people to the swimming hole after we cleaned the graves and placed our flowers. With so many hands to do this work, it was accomplished quickly.

I loaded my rented truckbed with as many people as would fit and asked my uncle to guide me while I drove. We slowly traveled through the pasture for about ten minutes and came upon the swimming hole. It was a large oval pond, about twenty feet long and fifteen feet across. There were large carp swimming in it. We all dove in and spent about thirty minutes swimming. We then heard Polynesian music playing over the PA system, so we loaded up the truck and returned to camp.

By this point, our numbers had swelled to more than 500 people. All the hula halau and entertainers with their families had arrived. It was the first time so many people had set foot on the land, but almost everyone was familiar with Iosepa's history.

After the first hula halau performed, I turned the time over to my uncle Lionel to share his memories about growing up in Iosepa. Having someone there who lived and grew up in the colony was an experience no one would forget. That is when I realized why I was called to lead SOPU.

After Uncle Lionel spoke, I took another group of swimmers to the swimming hole while my brother and our friends hosted the entertainment. The entertainment went nonstop late into the evening with groups from Utah, California, Hawaii, Arizona, and Nevada. We ate and celebrated late into the night, catching up with old friends and making new ones.

On Sunday, we gathered to hold our memorial service. God and the spirits of our ancestors were there as a gentle rain passed over us. We knew our efforts were appreciated and that being there at that sacred place was something we should continue.

This gathering was the largest Memorial Day gathering at Iosepa to that point. It drew the attention of many Polynesians on the Mainland and Hawaii, and from that point on, more families became involved in this tradition. With more people becoming involved, more improvements were made to the cemetery, which now includes a pavilion and a memorial headstone donated by Princess Abigail Kawananakoa, a member of the Hawaiian royal family. Iosepa is now a registered historical site. Visiting Iosepa during Memorial Day weekend has become engrained in many Polynesians who live in Hawaii, Utah, and Utah's surrounding states.

Why do reluctant leaders make the best leaders?

I believe reluctant leaders make the best leaders because they have no interest in power, prestige, or recognition. Their primary motive in stepping into a leadership role is to get the job done. Since they have no interest in cultivating power, they are more adaptable and creative in accomplishing the task. Once the task is completed, they have no problem in turning the leadership role over to someone else.

In "Are You a Reluctant Leader?" Walt Grassle writes: "often, reluctant leaders are the best leaders. They lead from a desire to serve, not a desire for power." And in "The Reluctant Leader," Lainie Heneghan writes: "Adaptability, humility, a capacity to bring others along in their efforts, and a plain old willingness to listen are defining qualities of reluctant leaders."

Strategies to support a reluctant leader

Since reluctant leaders still find their way into leadership roles, they can become more effective leaders by applying four strategies outlined by the CEO Warrior. (https://ceowarrior.com/4-leadership-strategies-for-reluctant-leaders/)

1. **Rely on Your Strengths.**

   As a skilled person in a trade, you are a problem solver. When you are faced with a job-related problem, you can think through the problem and identify cause and effect to discover a solution. These same skills apply to humans. Feel confident that you have navigated many problems and solutions before, and you can navigate this one too! Trust your ability as a problem solver.

2. **Set the Standard.**

   True leadership is setting the standard in everything you do. This is leading by example. Leaders are often disrespected or ignored because they adopt a "do what I say, not what I do" approach to leadership. But if you set a high standard and adhere to it always, the people you lead will notice your authenticity and they'll respect you, and that will give you the authority to direct them.

3. **Communicate Clearly.**

   Communicating clearly is a vital skill a leader must have. As a leader, you will be communicating with many people across all levels and in several different ways. You will be addressing owners, managers, colleagues, customers, suppliers, through memos, letters, or speaking with them. Each of these groups requires different information communicated in different ways. Your success as a leader is dependent on your ability to communicate effectively by relating information, giving direction, and negotiating.

4. **Multiply Yourself.**

   A good leader does not lead alone. You will need others to lead with you. When you are given a leadership role, start identifying other potential leaders that you can mentor to help take on some of the leadership burden. Encourage them to step up and take responsibility as a leader to begin leading others.

These four strategies will not be the magic pill to make all aspects of leadership easy, but they will give you a strong start and make this new position more successful.

Summary

In this chapter, we examined the reluctant leader and how people become reluctant leaders. We looked at two examples of reluctant leaders, Moses, and Cincinnatus, and then we examined my personal experiences as a reluctant leader. Finally, since many reluctant leaders do find themselves in leadership roles, we looked at four strategies that would help them become better leaders.

Exercise

Describe your first experience as a reluctant leader. What were the circumstances you or your organization faced? What motivated you to accept the role of leader?

_____

_____

_____

_____

_____

_____

What did you learn from your experiences as a reluctant leader? Will you take on a leadership role in the future? Why or why not?

___

A FINAL NOTE

We have now come to the end of our journey together in these pages, but I hope it is only the beginning of your new journey, filled with greater understanding about who you are, who you can be, and your soul's purpose.

In this book, you learned about the different types of journeys your soul can attract to your life to create the person you were meant to be. You learned that near-death experiences are gateways to developing new spiritual abilities and insights. You saw how my first NDE triggered my ability to communicate with spirits and see objects hidden from view. You also learned you could develop your natural talents and abilities and expand them to other areas. You then learned through my second NDE that there is a place called heaven where you can be reunited with your family members and pets. After establishing contact with your ancestors and knowing who they are, you can find ways to talk with them if you so desire. Through my third NDE, you learned that death is not as final as you may think. Many times, you need to face death to appreciate the life you have. You were then introduced to concepts of energy healing and remote viewing. Through my fourth and final NDE, you learned the important role of your spirit guides in protecting you when you are spiritually and physically threatened. In the closing sections of this book, I included some instructional materials for Ha Ki'i Healing and Medical Intuition, as well as a method I use to make predictions on sporting events. I then ended by sharing my work as a kahu and psychic and my personal approach to leadership.

If you apply the knowledge, experiences, skills, and strategies I offered in this book to your life, you will achieve peace and balance in your soul's journey.

Now that you have read my book and had the opportunity to complete the exercises, what steps are you prepared to take at this point to place you on your path to happiness and fulfilment?

I challenge you to act now. Having knowledge does not give you the power to change. You must apply knowledge to obtain power.

In the exercise lines below, list ten actions you will commit to doing in the next ninety days to get in touch with your soul.

1. _____
2. _____
3. _____
4. _____
5. _____
6. _____
7. _____
8. _____
9. _____
10. _____

Now that you have read my book, I encourage you to contact me and tell me what you liked and did not like about this book so I can improve it for the next printing. More importantly, tell me more about you, your challenges, your obstacles, and your adversities so I can help you. I would like to offer you a complimentary 30-60-minute consultation by phone to see if I can help you.

My email address is davidjwallace04@gmail.com and my cell phone number is (808) 349-4788. Email or text me your name and time zone, and we will schedule your complimentary consultation.

I wish you good luck and safe journeys in all you do. I wish you success, prosperity, and a happy soul's journey.

ABOUT THE AUTHOR

David J. Wallace is an author, professional keynote speaker, educator, kahu, reiki master, remote viewer, seer, Native Hawaiian cultural practitioner, medical intuitive, and psychic intuitive. He is the founder of Ha Ki'i Healing and Medical Intuition Methodology and developer of the Picking Winner$ Method of predicting the future. He offers training workshops in healing, medical intuition, predicting sporting events, and choosing winning roulette and lottery numbers.

Kahu Wallace is a retired high school social studies teacher with a BA in Teaching Social Studies, with emphasis in history and psychology, from BYU Hawaii. He has also earned advanced certifications in psychology, an MS degree in Public Administration from the University of Hawaii, and a Master's of Metaphysical Science and Divinity from the Metaphysical University. He is currently a doctoral candidate in Metaphysical Science.

Kahu Wallace was born on the island of Molokai, Hawaii. He was raised in the Hawaiian Homestead community of Ho'olehua and has been immersed in Hawaiian culture since childhood. After injuring his head by falling out of a moving vehicle, Kahu Wallace began to develop the first of many different skills that followed these brushes with death.

Kahu Wallace is a descendant of ruling chiefs, kahunas, healers, seers, seafarers, navigators, explorers, educators, fishermen, farmers, and warriors. From an early age, he learned to communicate with these ancestors through dreams, visions, and visitations. His ancestors tutored and inspired Kahu Wallace to develop his natural abilities and reach beyond his limitations.

ABOUT DAVID J. WALLACE'S COACHING PROGRAM

If you want to discover, develop, and maximize your natural abilities so you can realize your soul purpose in life, then finding the right coach to help you achieve your goals should be your top priority. Having the right coach, someone who has walked the walk and understands your struggles and frustrations, will help ease your growing pains.

Let author, educator, psychic, remote viewer, healer, and medical intuitive, Kahu David J. Wallace guide you through the process of discovering, developing, and maximizing your natural abilities. Since 2014, Kahu David has guided hundreds of clients in establishing their individual practices in several different fields. These fields include psychic readers, educators, counselors, medical intuitives, workshop presenters, healers, energy workers, advantage gamers, and remote viewers. He has also helped enhance the abilities of well-established practitioners.

Take advantage of Kahu David's specialized talents and abilities today.

To schedule a complimentary, no-obligation 30-60-minute consultation by phone, email Kahu David at davidjwallace04@gmail.com or text him with your name and time zone at (808) 349-4788.

SEMINARS, WORKSHOPS, AND TRAINING

You can learn to be a healer, medical intuitive, remote viewer, and advantage gamer by enrolling in David J. Wallace's seminars and workshops, held in Hawaii and via video conferencing. These seminars and workshops are scheduled monthly or can be scheduled on demand by appointment. The following classes are offered:

HA KI'I HEALING & MEDICAL INTUITION

Learn to be an energy healer and medical intuitive by enrolling in our three workshops. These workshops are designed to provide the energy worker with the skills needed to harness and use pure healing energy to heal and conduct medical scans as a medical intuitive.

- *Ha Ki'i Healing*
  This one-day workshop teaches the energy worker how to tap into a pure energy source you can use to heal yourself and others. You will learn to assemble a team of spiritual helpers who will serve as your healing team while you are conducting a healing session. You will also learn a way to cleanse yourself of negative forces that could interfere with your health and wellbeing.

- *Ha Ki'i Medical Intuition 1*
  This one-day workshop serves as an introduction to the field of medical intuition. The class' focus will be developing your ability to sense energy in the human body so you can locate and then

describe the source of pain or illness in a person. You will be introduced to reiki and remote viewing and be given practice time to use your developing skills.

- ***Ha Ki'i Medical Intuition 2***
  This one-day workshop continues your medical intuition training. This time, you will learn how to perform a medical scan by using a proxy. This knowledge will allow you to conduct scans on anyone around the world.

HA KI'I CERTIFIED PRACTITIONER

This rigorous training program can lead to official certification as a Ha Ki'i practitioner. Candidates will be required to enroll in all the Ha Ki'i courses and skills courses, and successfully complete a one-year apprenticeship program with the Ha Ki'i Master. Candidates must also pass a final examination and demonstration of skills to receive their certification. Ha Ki'i instructors will be picked from those who excel in this program. Non-certificate-seeking participants are welcome to enroll in any of these workshops.

GAMING WORKSHOPS

Learn to be an advantage gamer by learning the best methods and strategies to play the casino games of your choice. David J. Wallace's workshops for gaming are focused on the following casino games: 4-card keno, slot machines, roulette, and craps. He also offers training in predicting sports and picking winning numbers for the lottery.

For more details and a free 30-60-minute consultation regarding David J. Wallace's workshops and seminars, contact him with your name and time zone via email, davidjwallace04@gmail.com or by calling (808) 349-4788.

BOOK KAHU DAVID J. WALLACE TO SPEAK AT YOUR NEXT EVENT

When it comes to choosing a professional speaker for your next event, you will find no one more respected or successful than Kahu David J. Wallace, one of the most gifted speakers of our generation. Since 2015, Kahu David J. Wallace has delivered more than 200 inspirational presentations in the United States, some of which have aired on the radio, internet, and television.

Whether your audience is 10 or 10,000, in the United States or abroad, Kahu David can deliver a customized message for your meeting or conference. Kahu David understands your audience does not want to be taught anything, but is interested in hearing stories of inspiration, achievement, and real-life people stepping into their destinies.

As a result, Kahu David's speaking philosophy is to humor, entertain, and inspire your audience with passion and stories proven to help people achieve extraordinary results. If you are looking for a memorable speaker who will leave your audience wanting more, book Kahu David J. Wallace today!

To view a highlight video of Kahu David J. Wallace and find out if he is available for your next meeting, visit his website at the address below. Then contact him by phone or email to schedule a complimentary pre-speech phone interview:

www.TheJourneyofOurSouls.com

davidjwallace04@gmail.com

(808) 349-4788

www.ingramcontent.com/pod-product-compliance
Lightning Source LLC
Chambersburg PA
CBHW071657090426
42738CB00009B/1557